Classic Cars of the 1950's

By Jordan Biggio

As a bonus each classic automobile design is listed twice in this book. Not only does this give you the opportunity to color each scene twice, it also gives you a clean slate in case you make a mistake! It is like having two copies of the same book.

As a second bonus, both the front and back cover are printed with a matte finish. This means you can color them too!

Thank you for purchasing a copy of my book. I had a great time creating this book for you and I would to see what you do with the designs. Feel free to email me images of what you have colored. My email address is:

jordanbiggio@gmail.com

If you enjoyed coloring my designs, then please leave a review to let others know what you thought, be it good or bad. Leaving a review is the single best way to help support me and my art. Leaving a review is easy and don't forget to post a completed colored page with your review.

Thanks again!

Jordan

ISBN-13: 978-1-945803-13-0
ISBN-10: 1-945803-13-4

A Sample of What's Inside

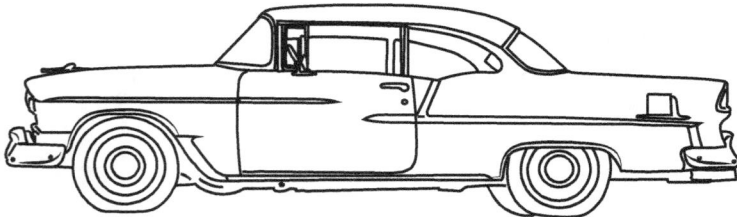

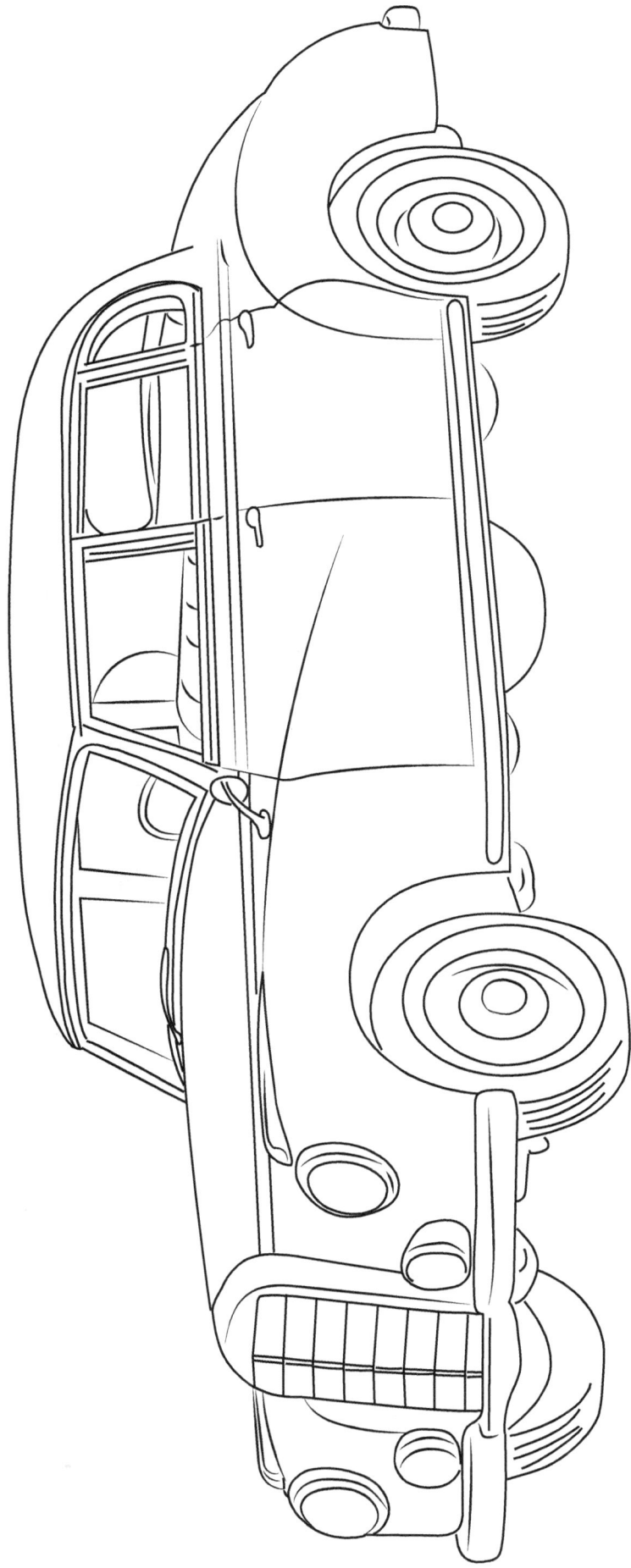

1951 Mercedes Benz Type 300

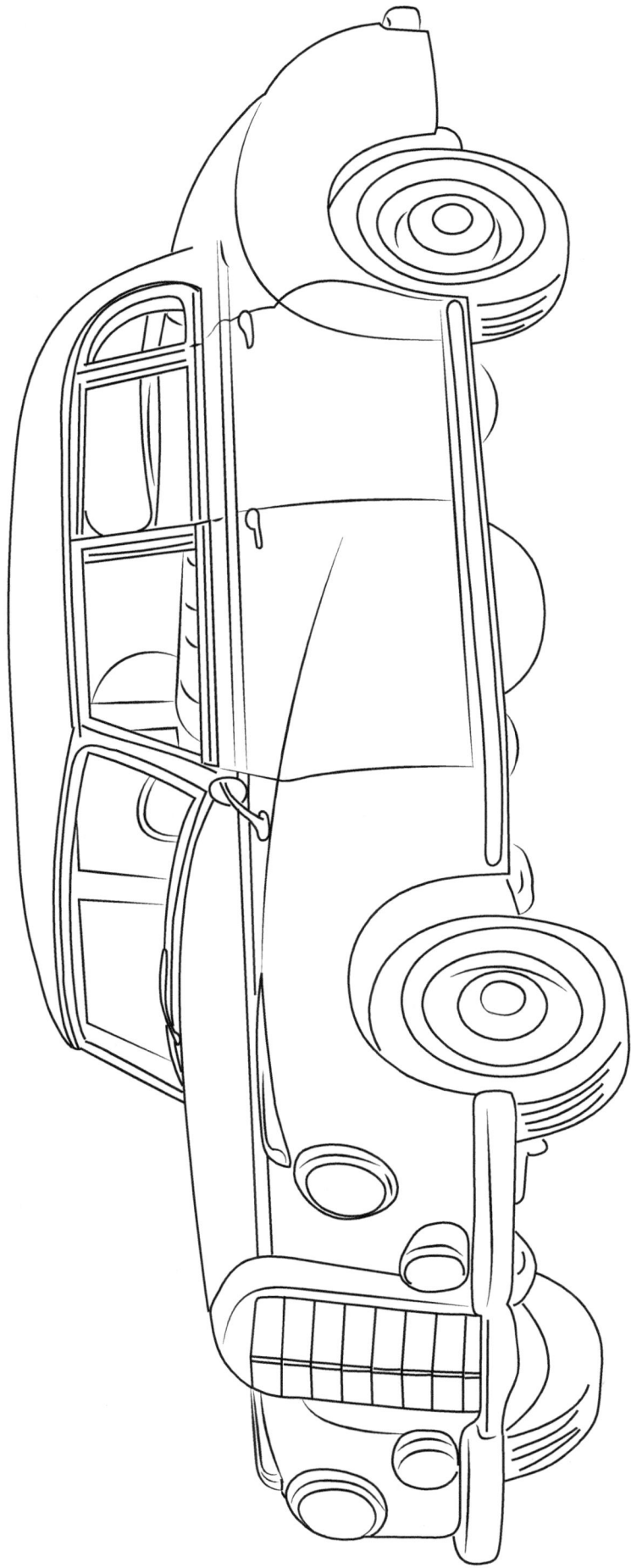

1951 Mercedes Benz Type 300

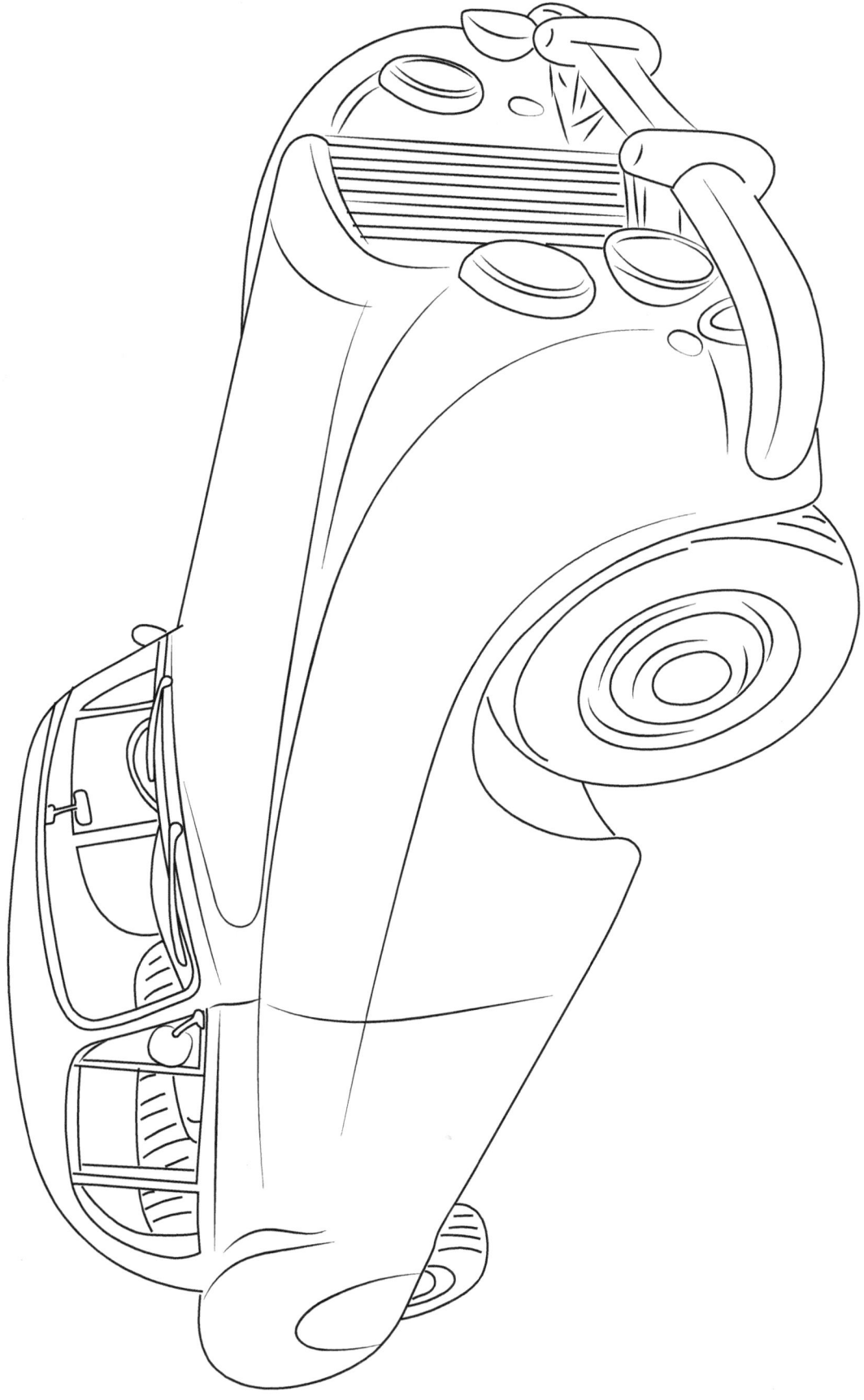

1952 Bentley R Type Continental

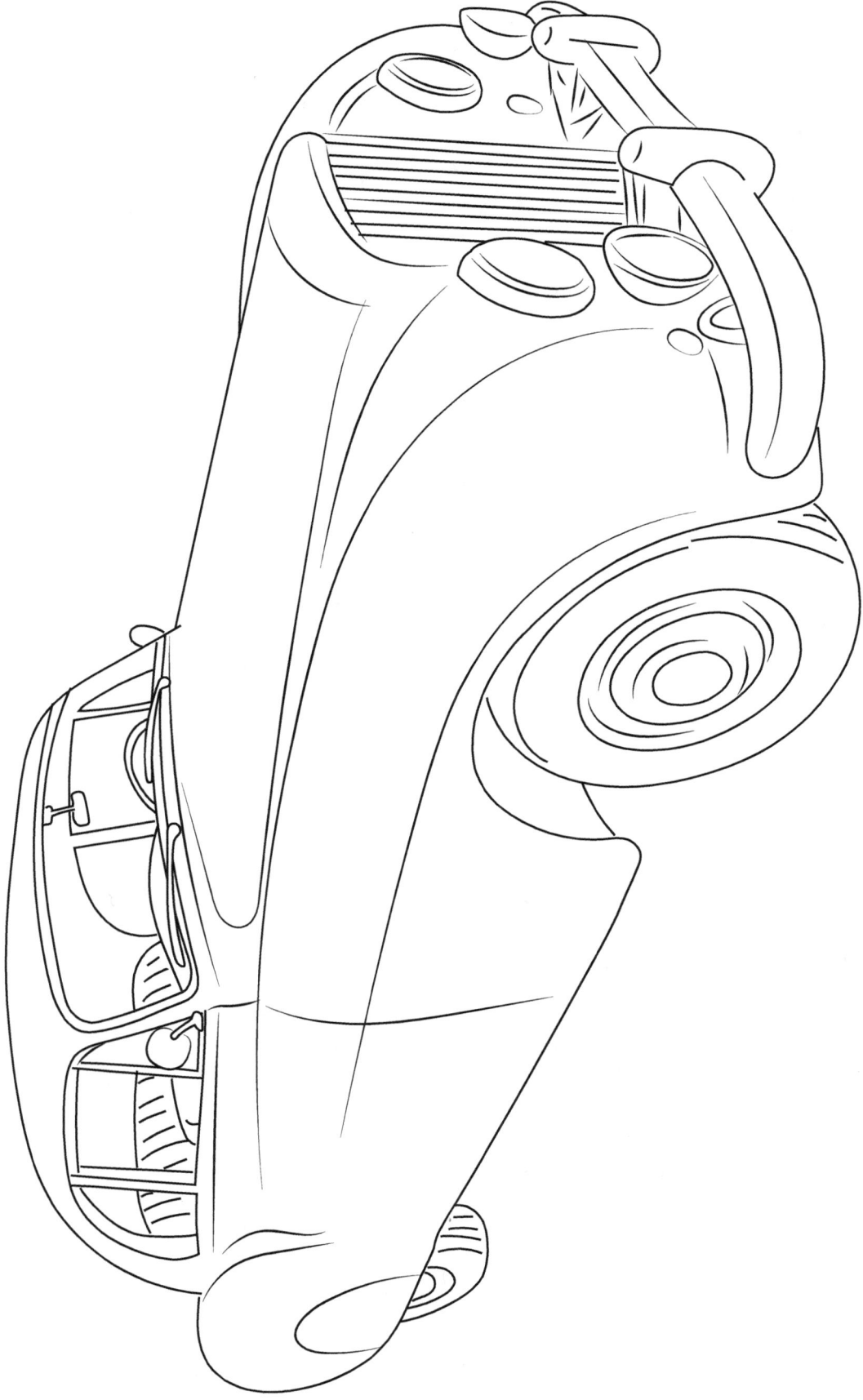

1952 Bentley R Type Continental

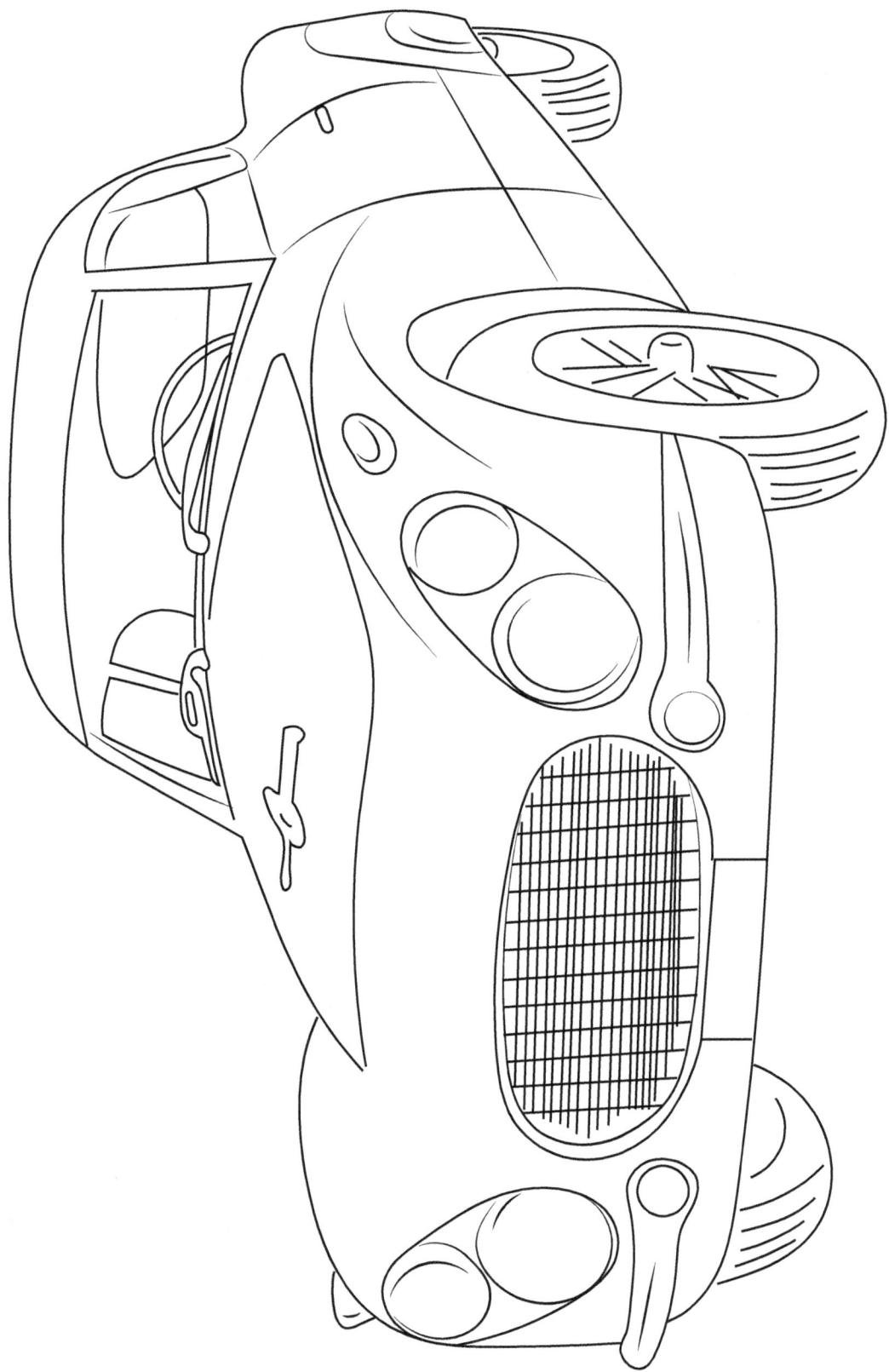

1952 FIAT 8V

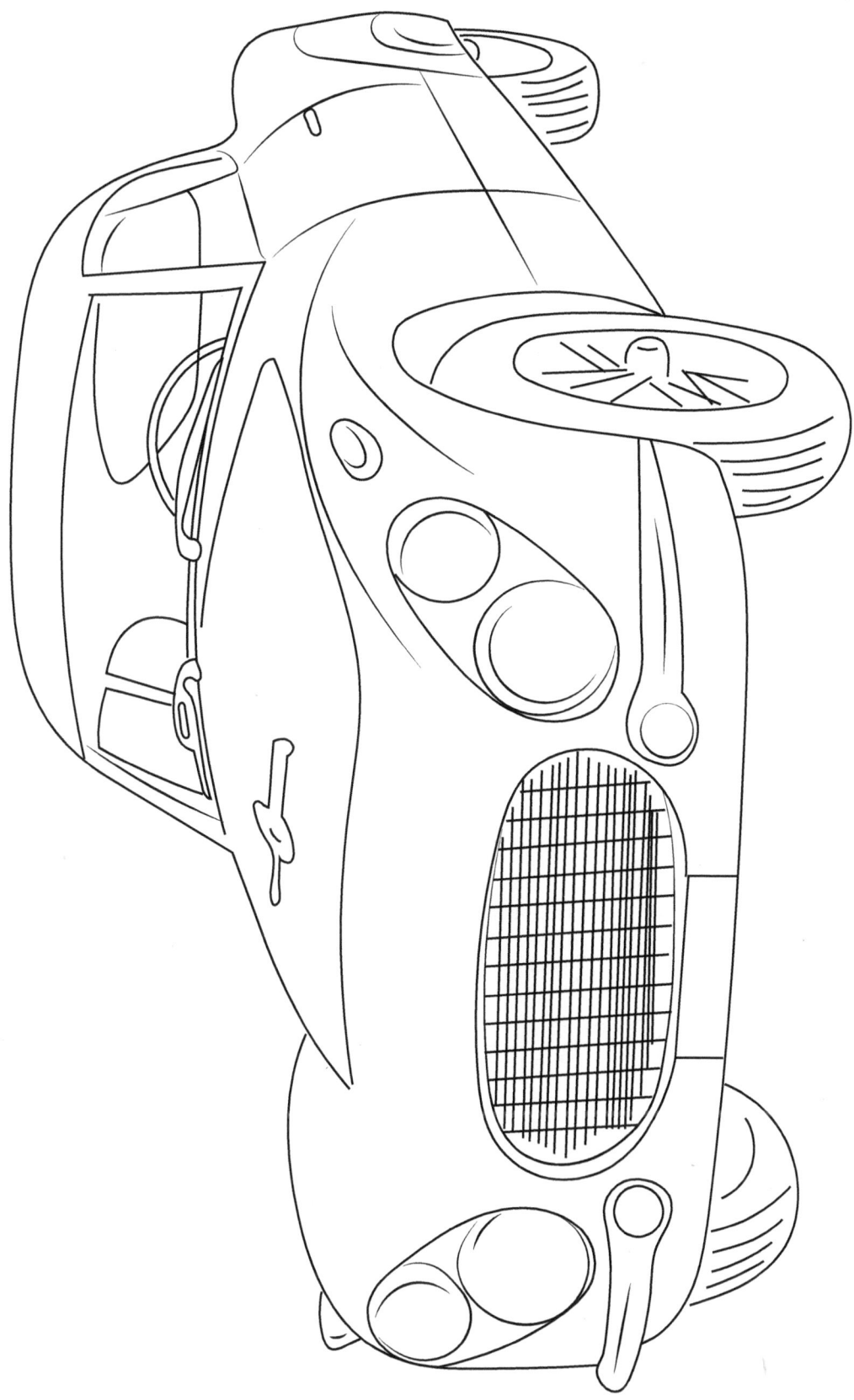

1952 FIAT 8V

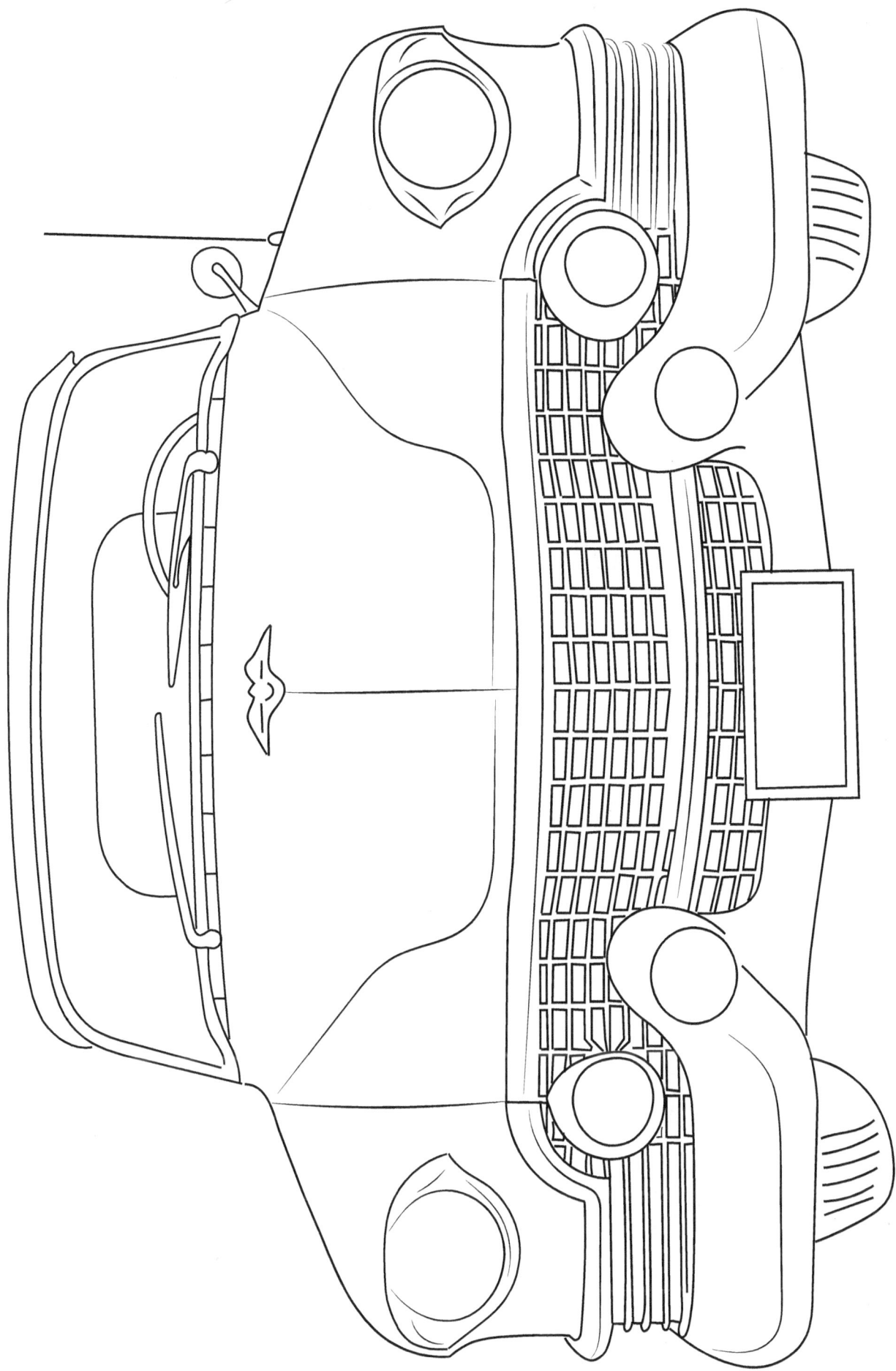

1954 Cadillac Eldorado

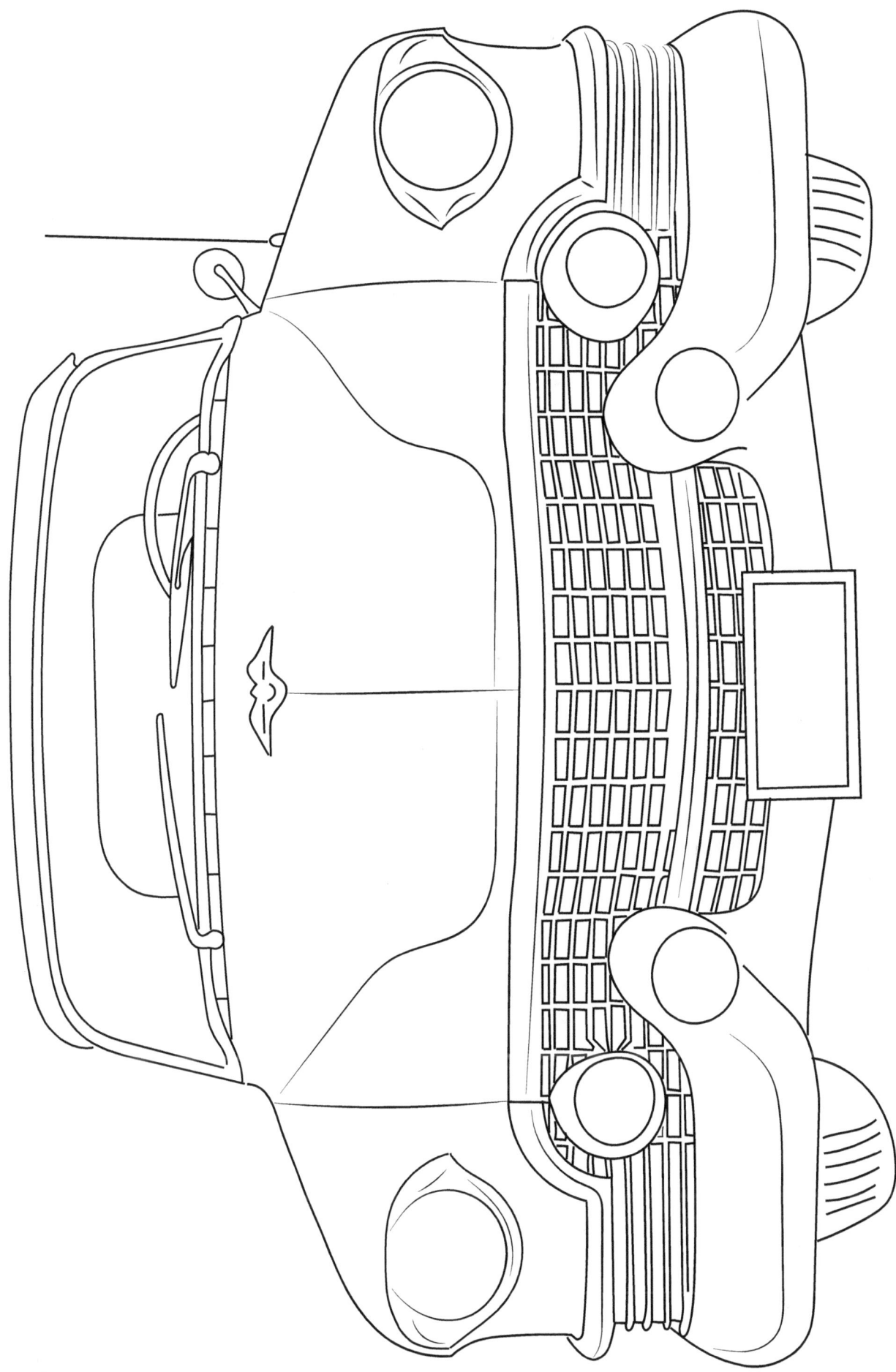

1954 Cadillac Eldorado

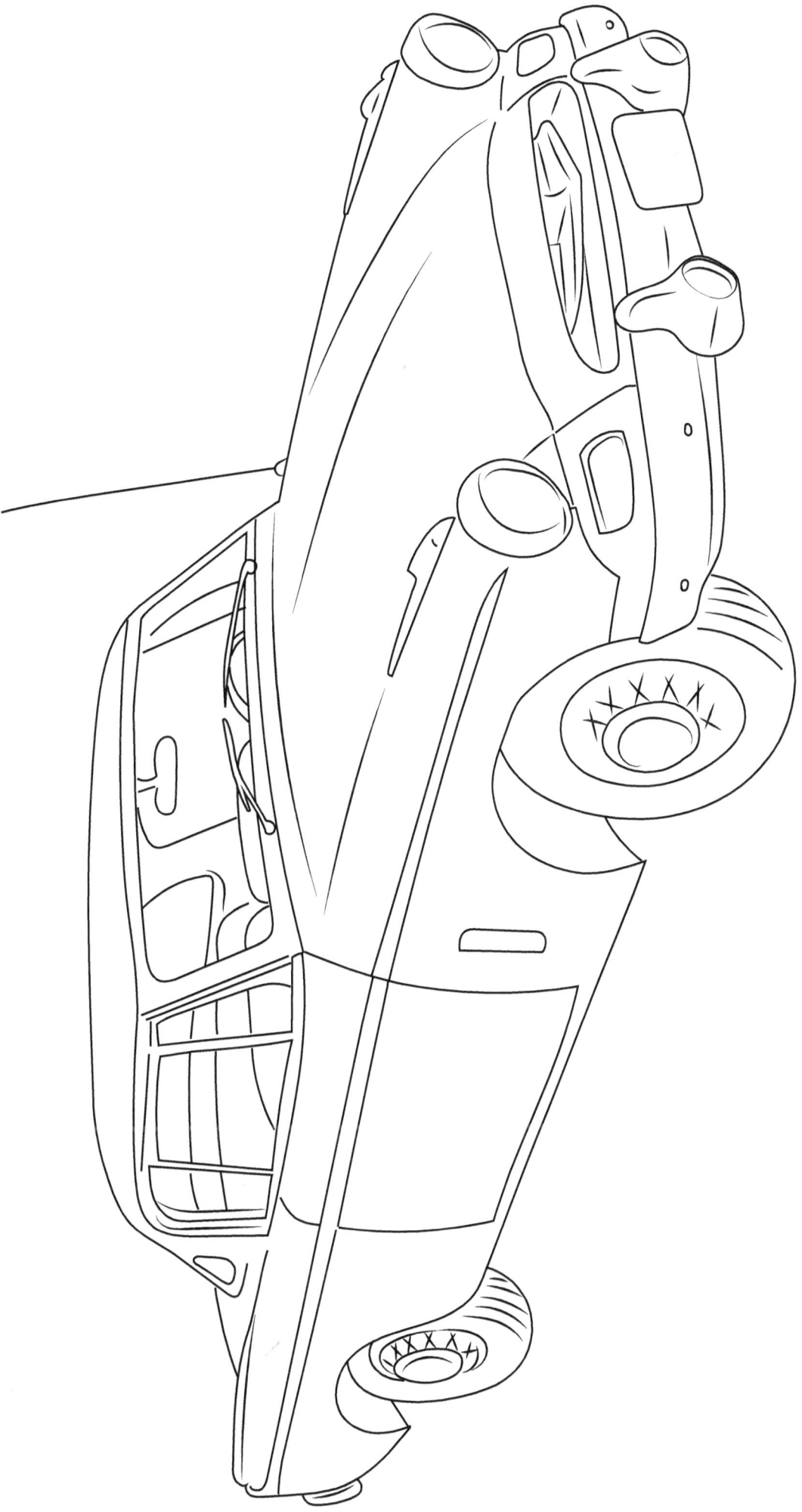

1955 Studebaker President Speedster

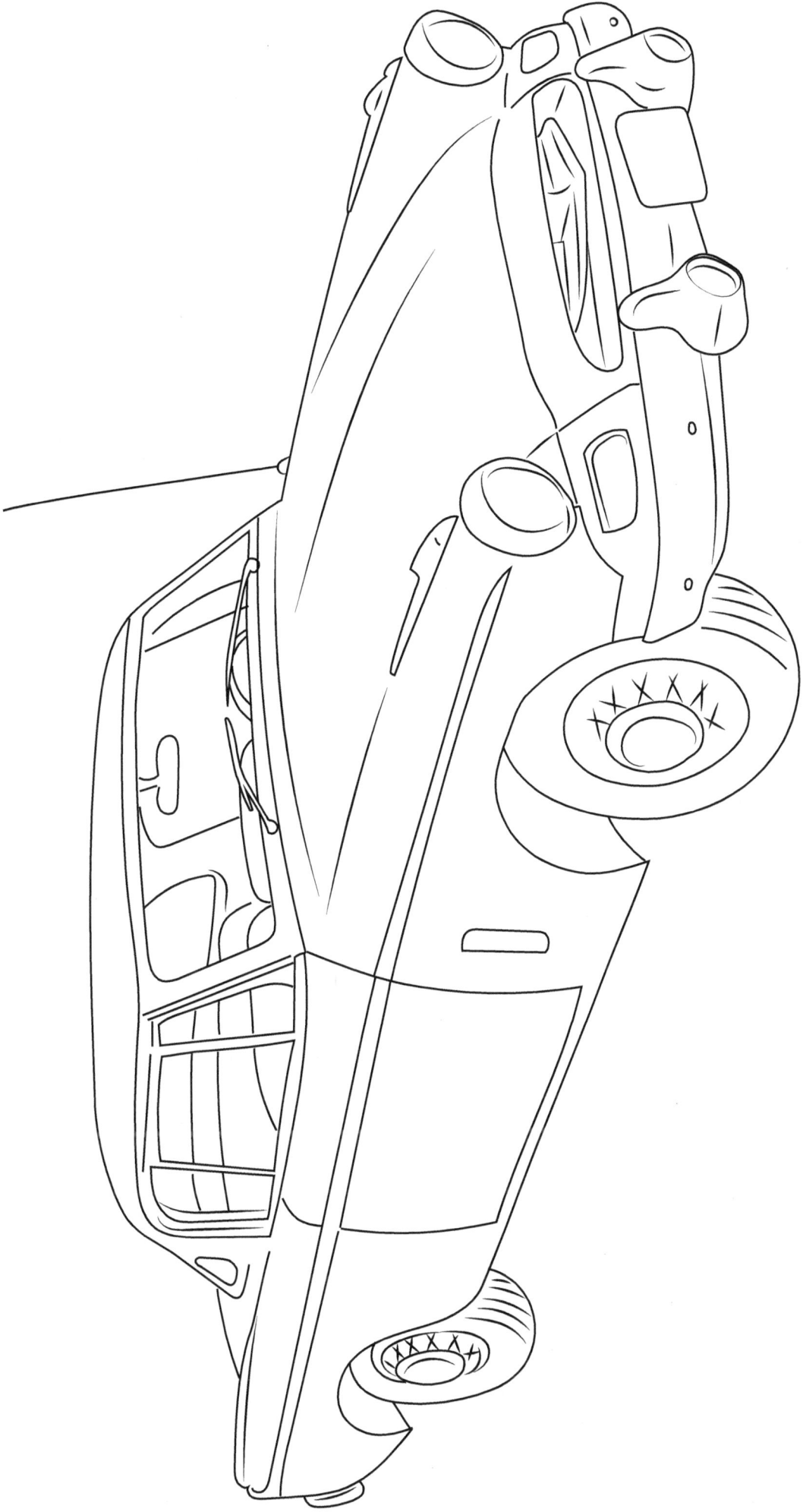

1955 Studebaker President Speedster

1955 Buick Skylark

1955 Buick Skylark

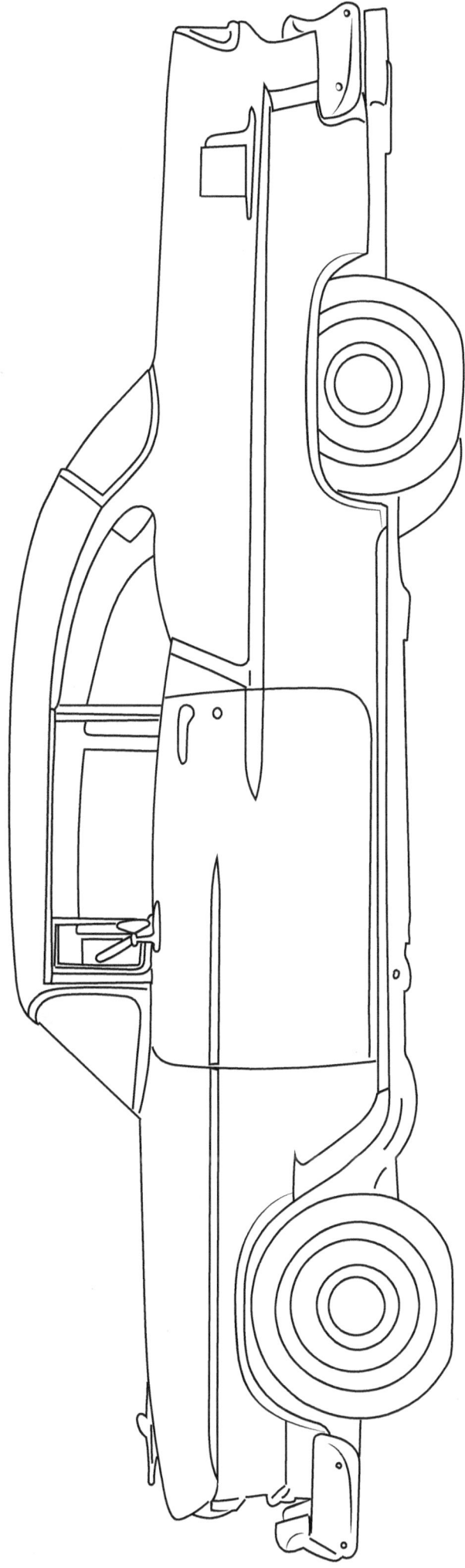

1955 Chevy Bel Air

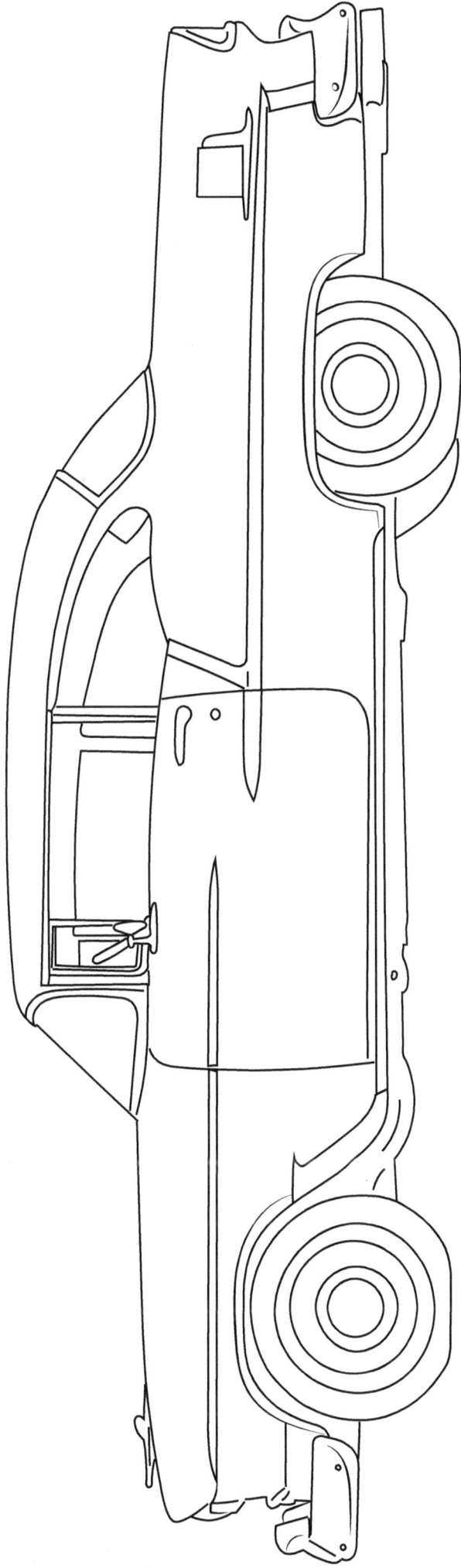

1955 Chevy Bel Air

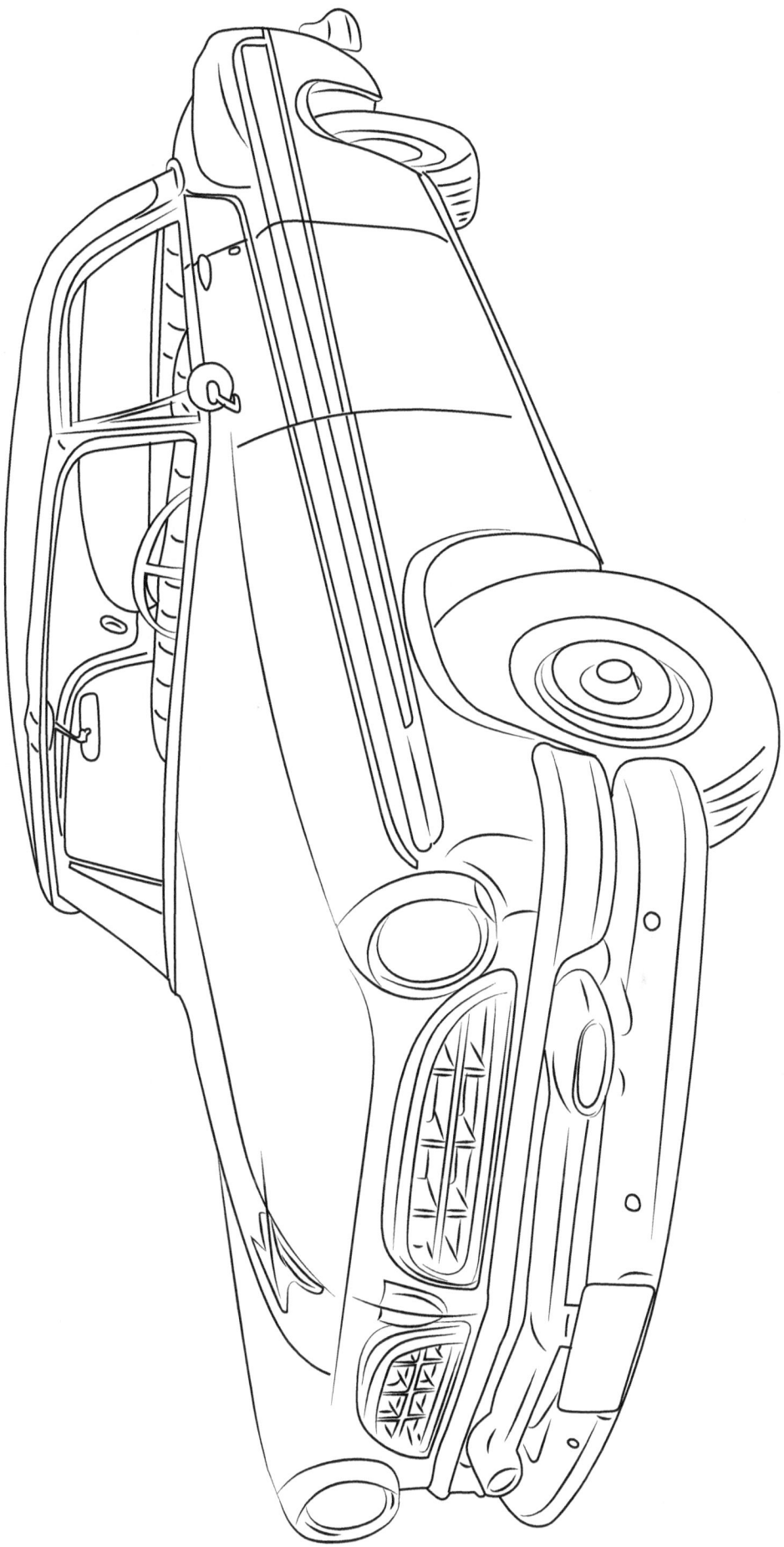

1955 Chrysler New Yorker

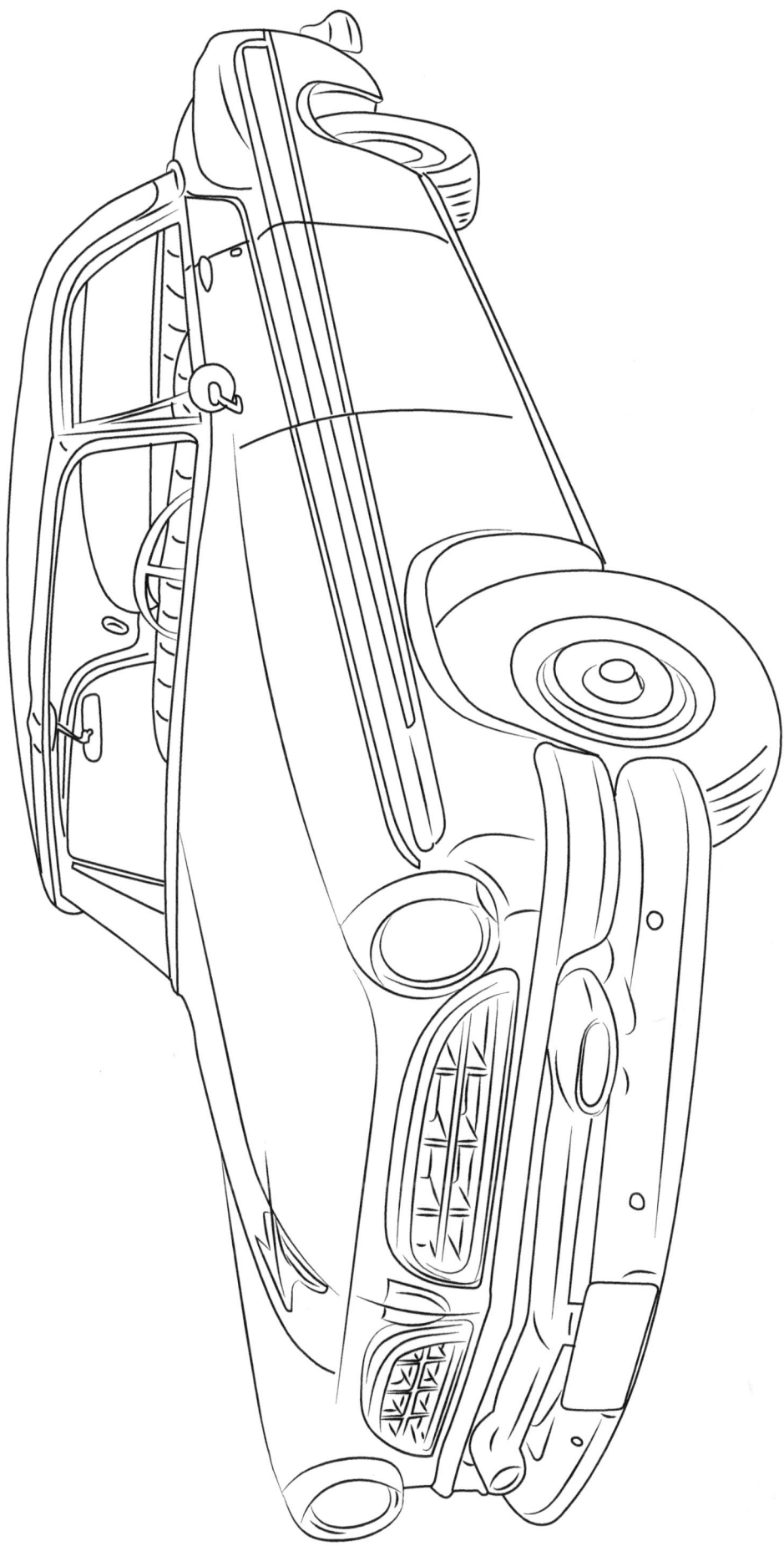

1955 Chrysler New Yorker

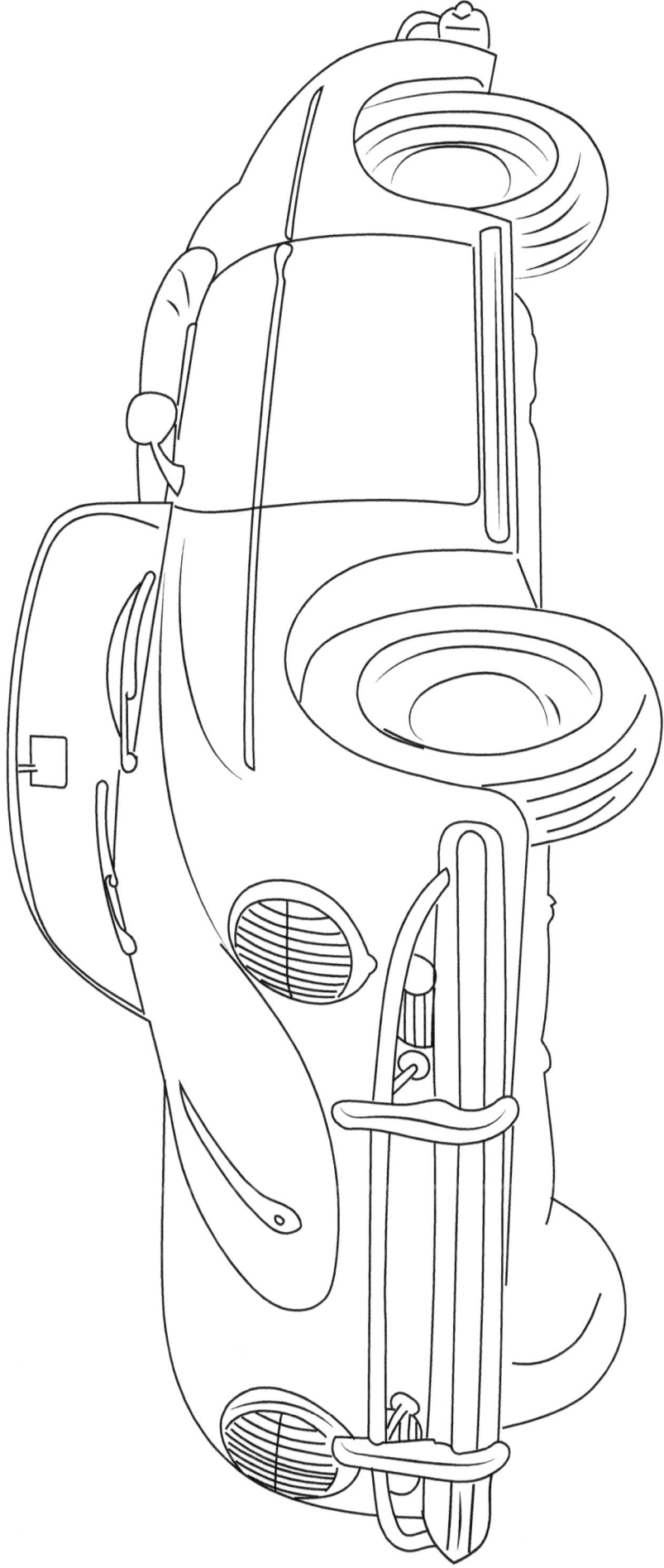

1955 Porsche 356 Roadster

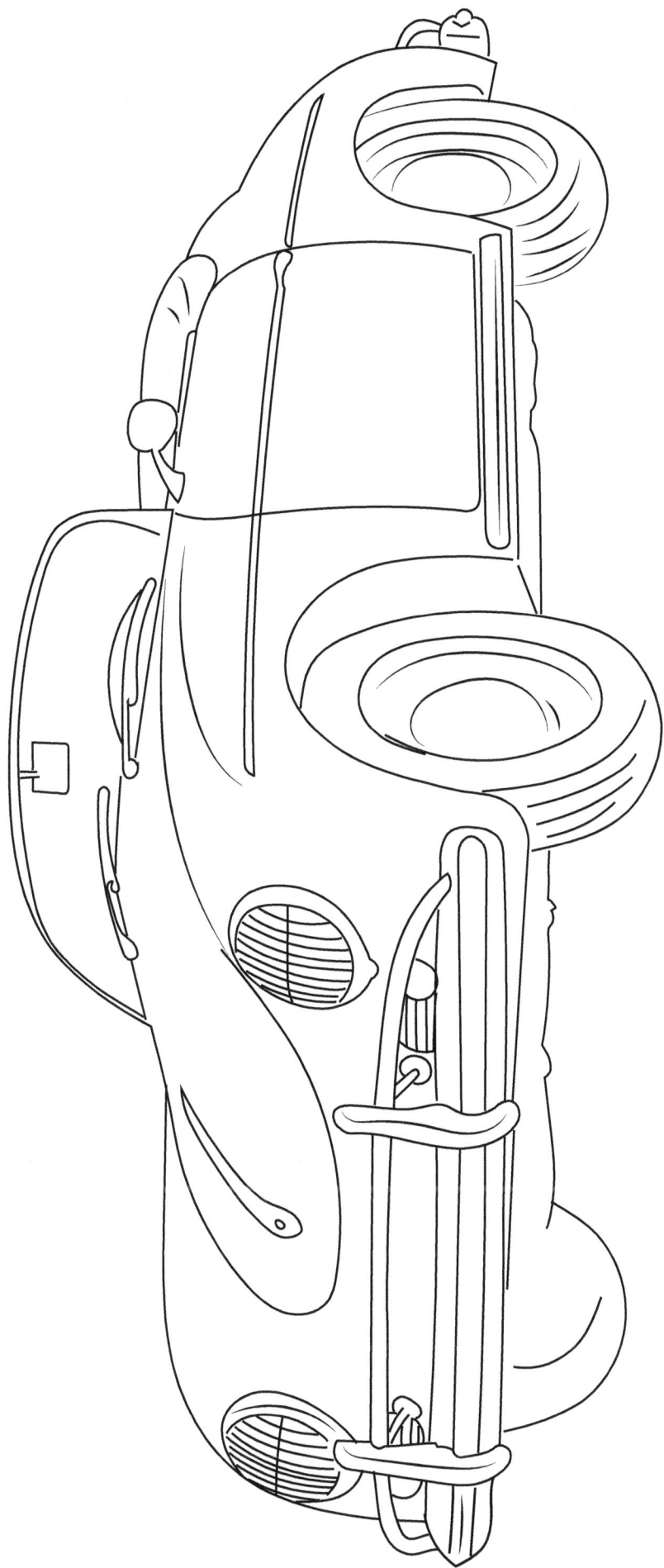

1955 Porsche 356 Roadster

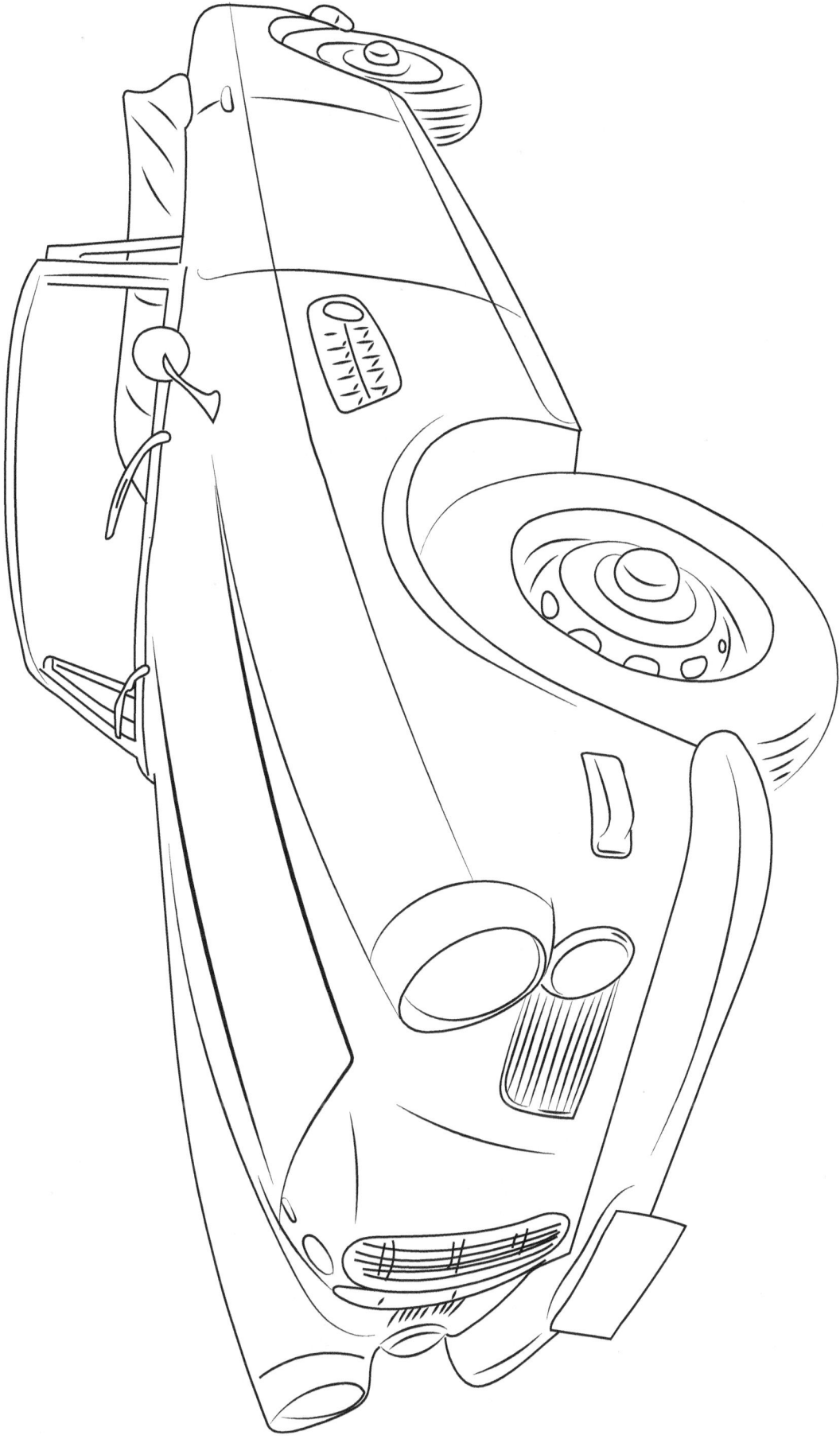

1956 BMW 503

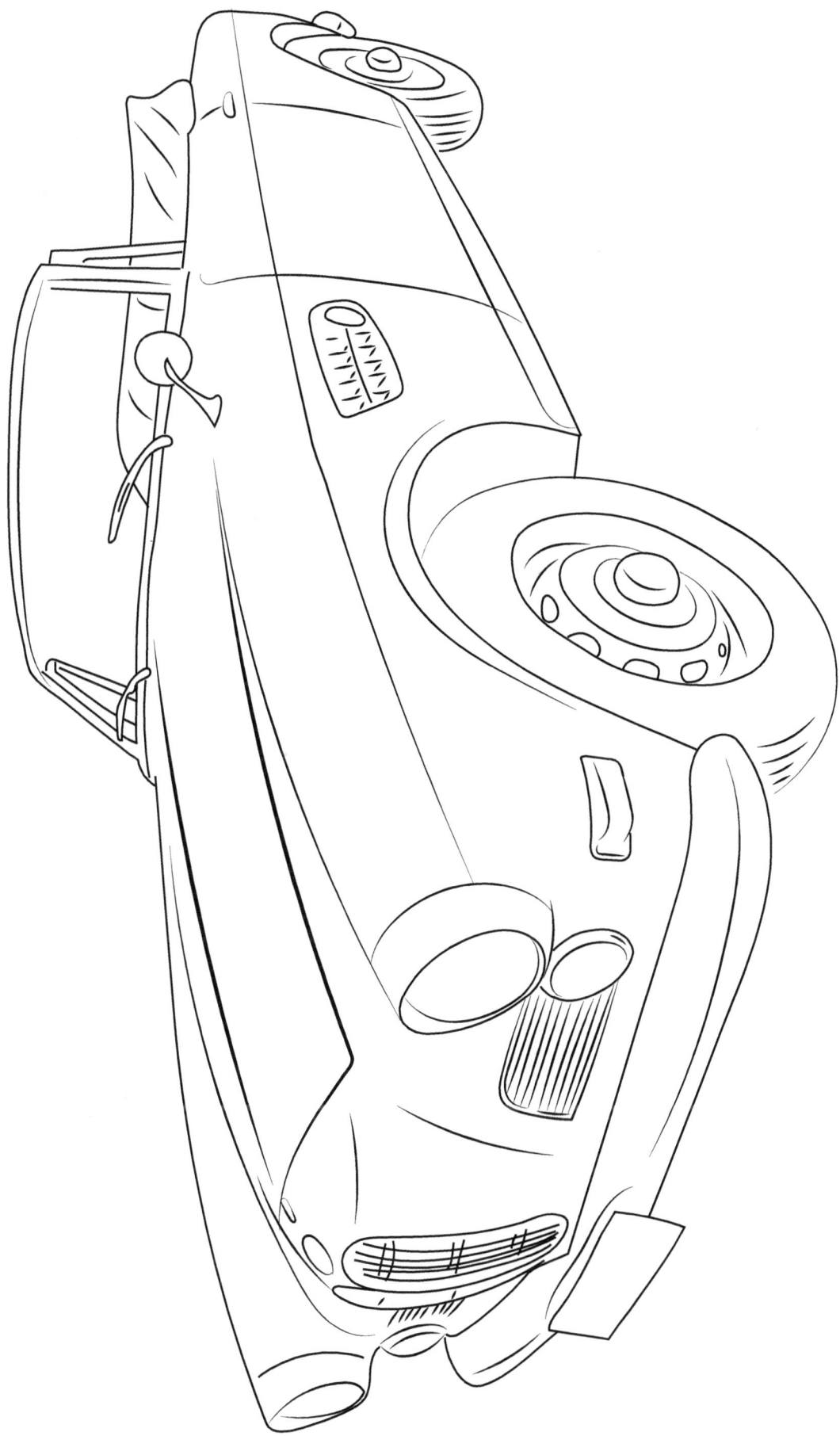

1956 BMW 503

1956 Chrysler Imperial

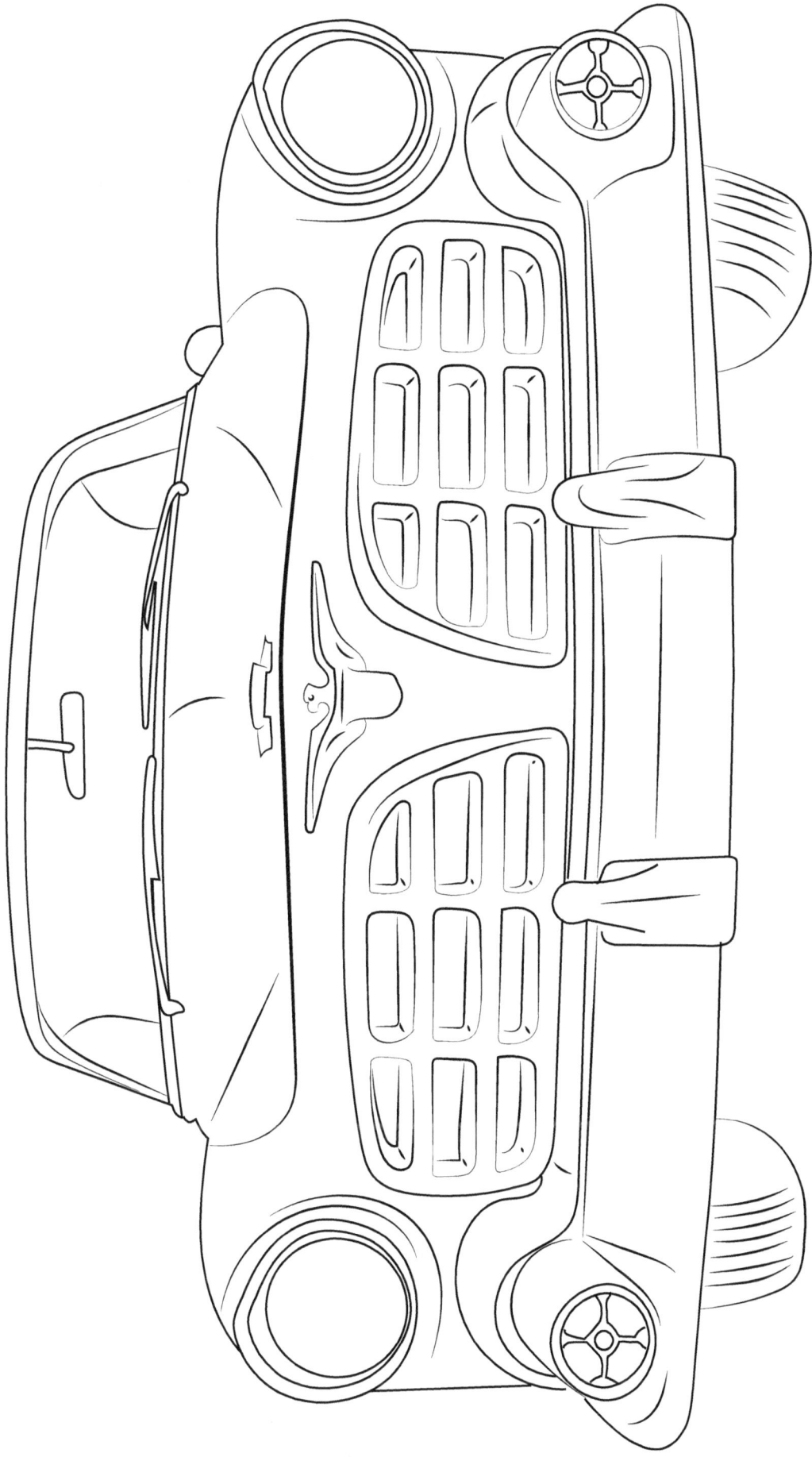

1956 Chrysler Imperial

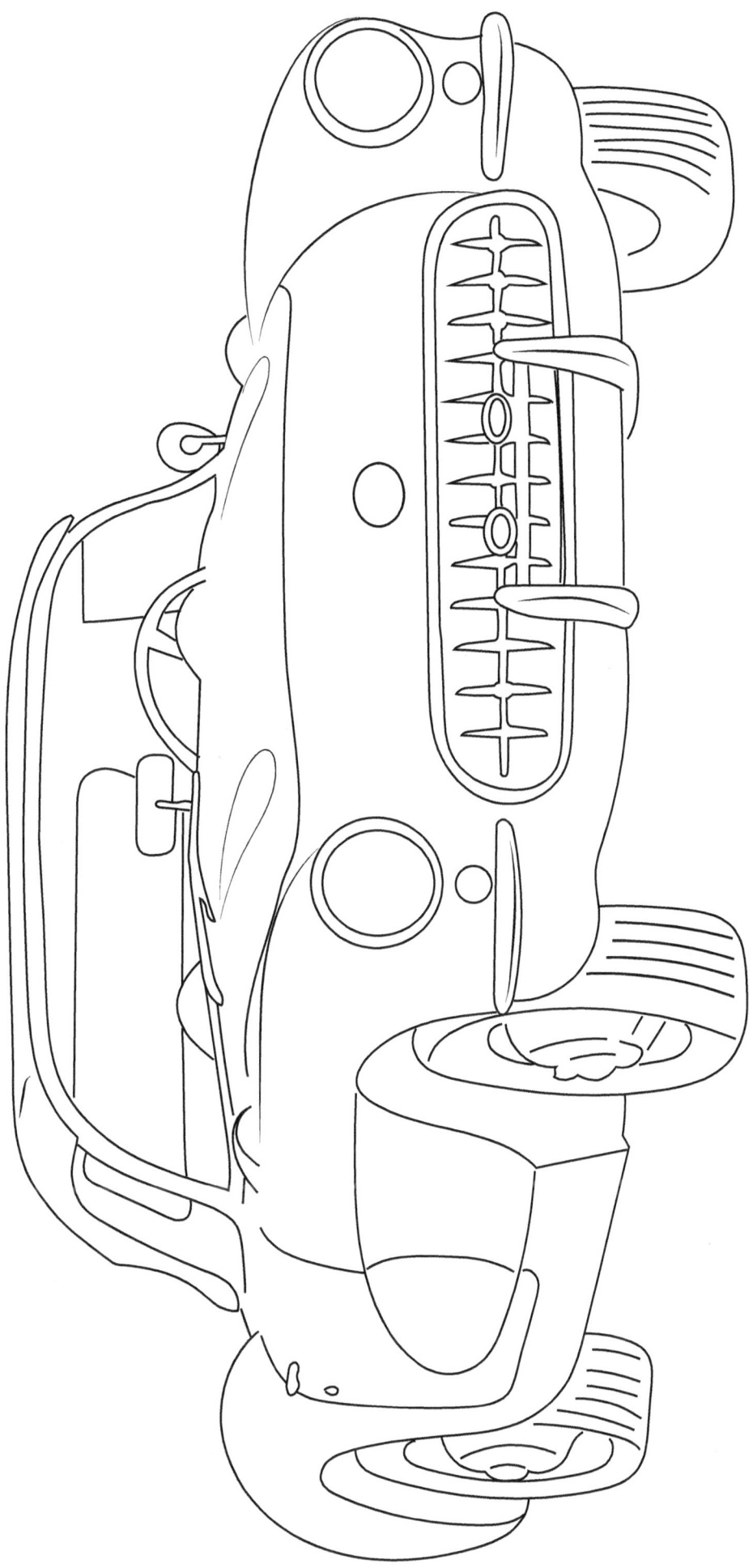

1957 Chevy Corvette

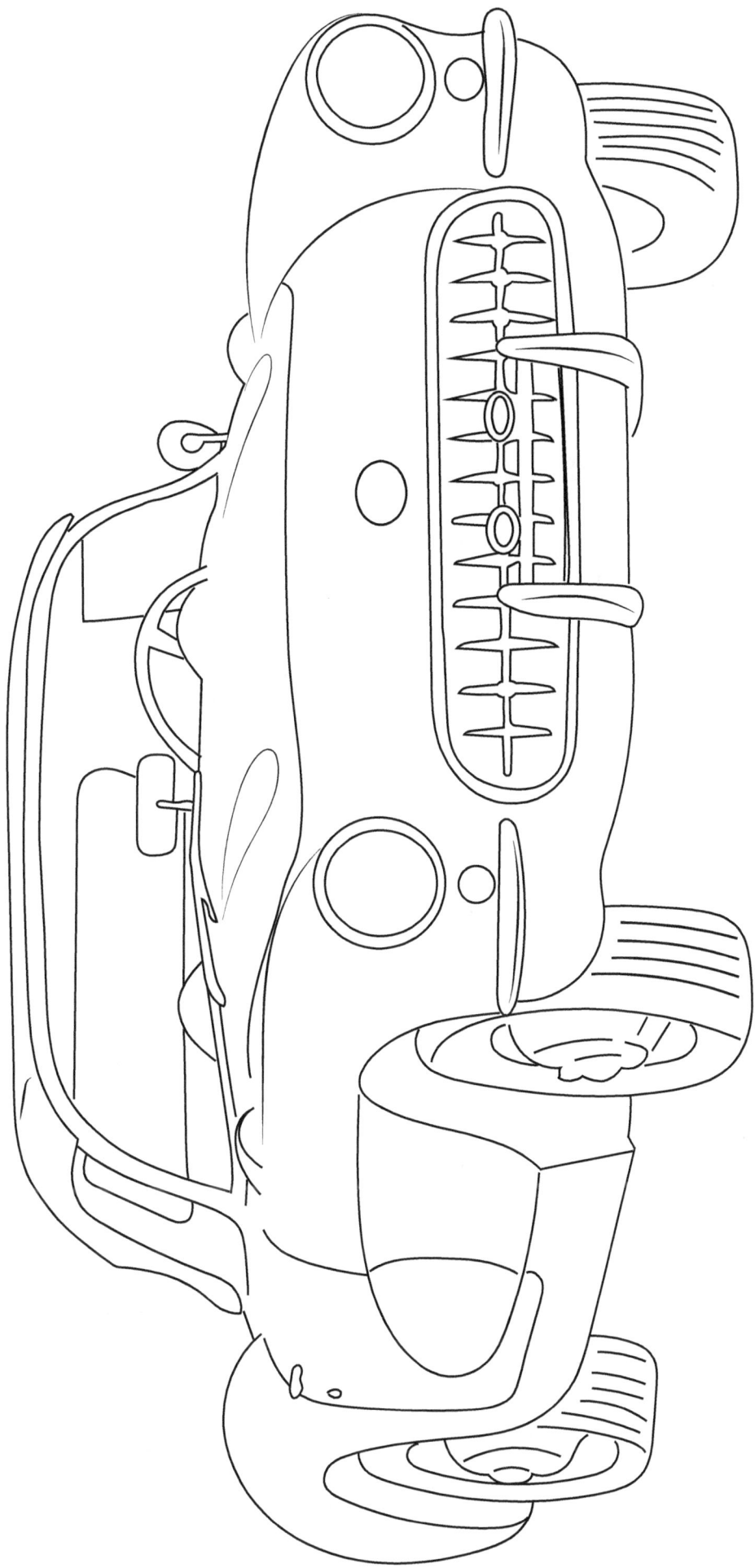

1957 Chevy Corvette

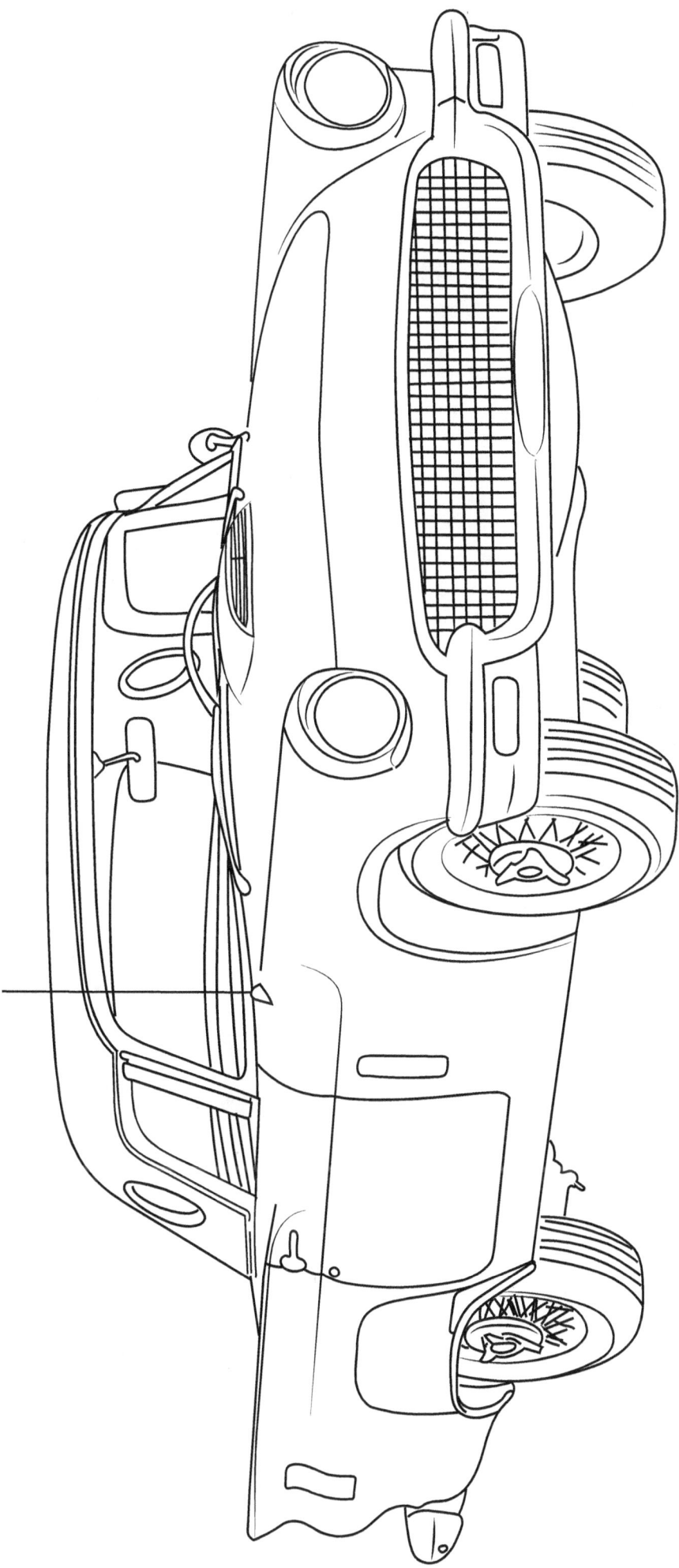

1957 Ford Thunderbird

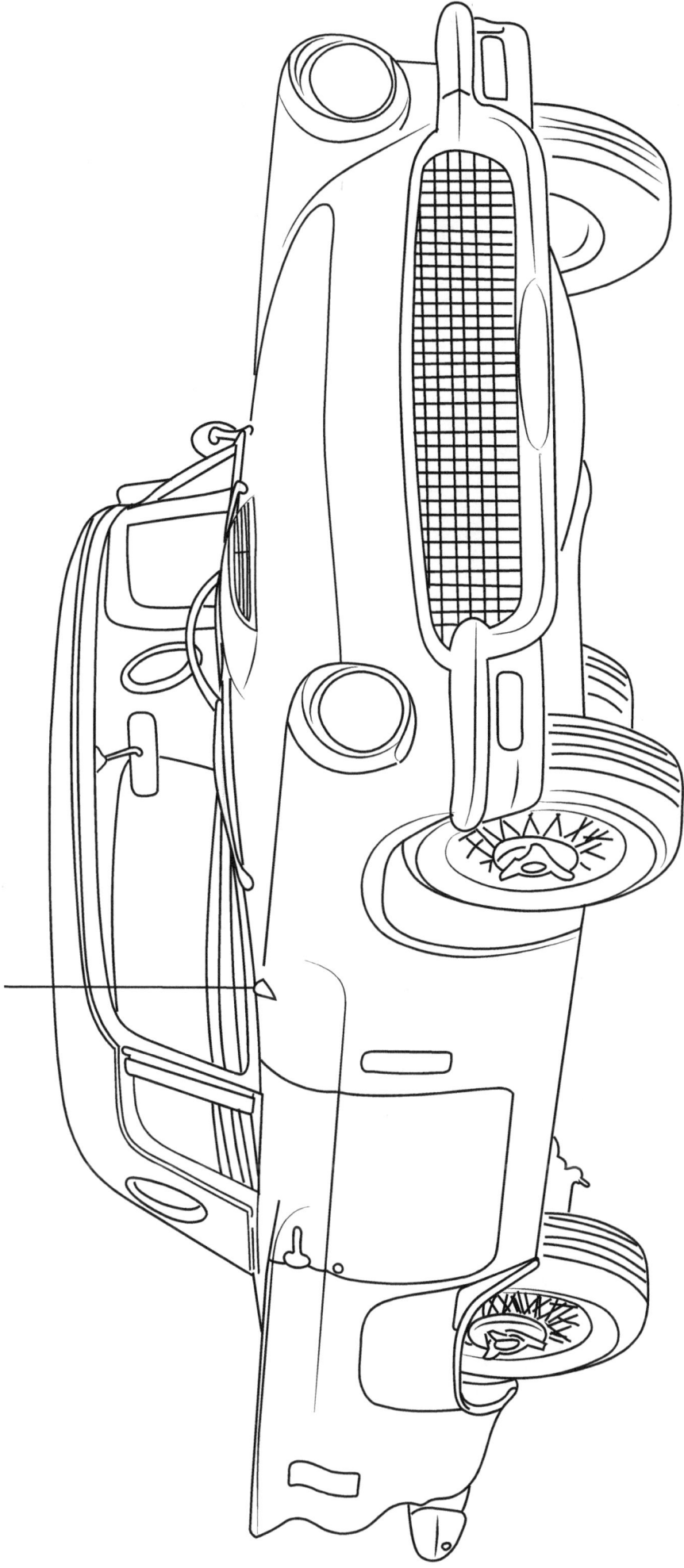

1957 Ford Thunderbird

1958 Buick Limited

1958 Buick Limited

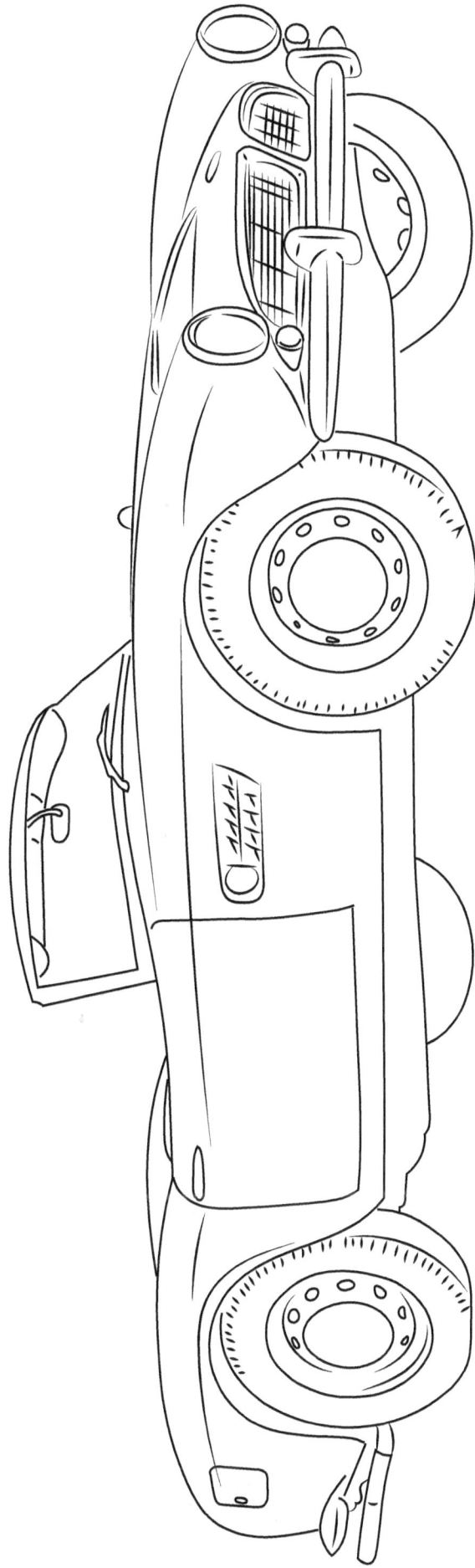

1958 BMW 507 Roadster

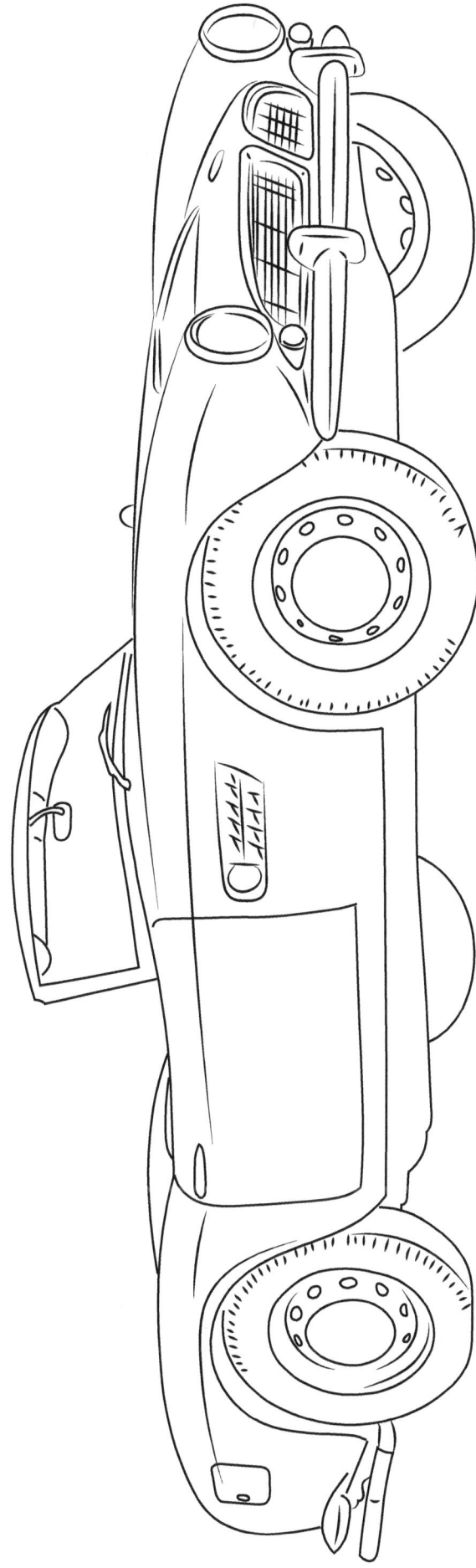

1958 BMW 507 Roadster

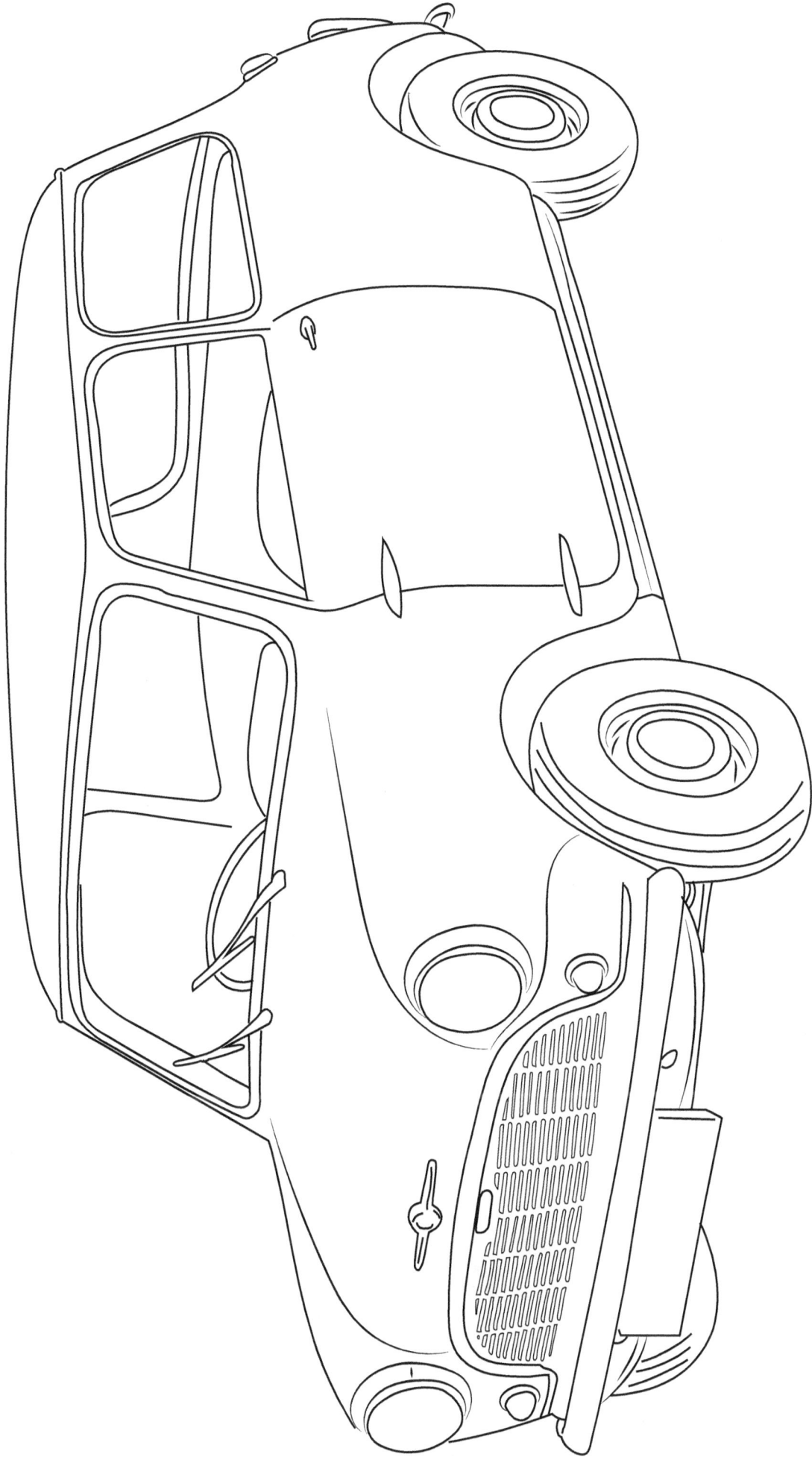

1959 Austin Mini

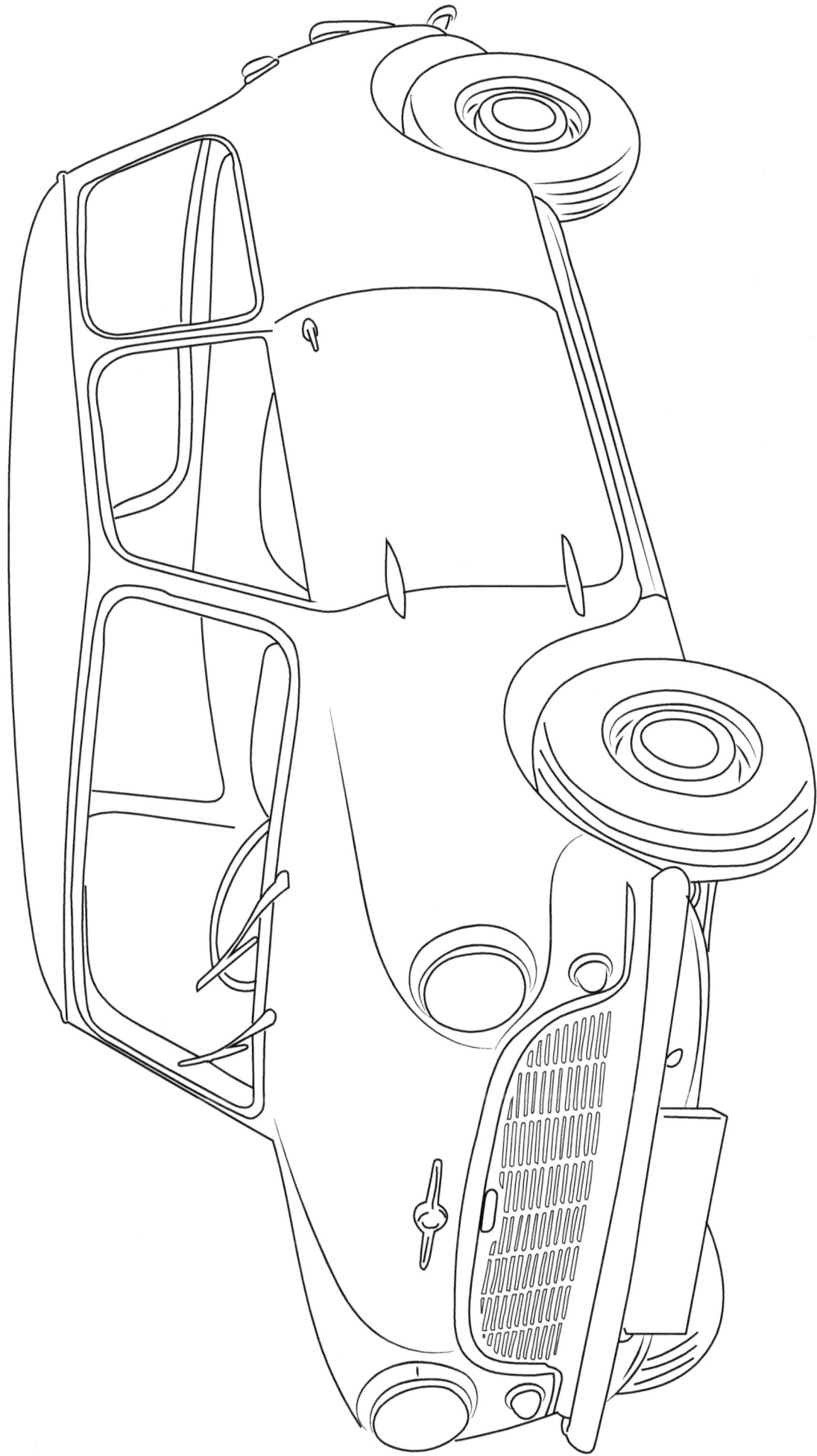

1959 Austin Mini

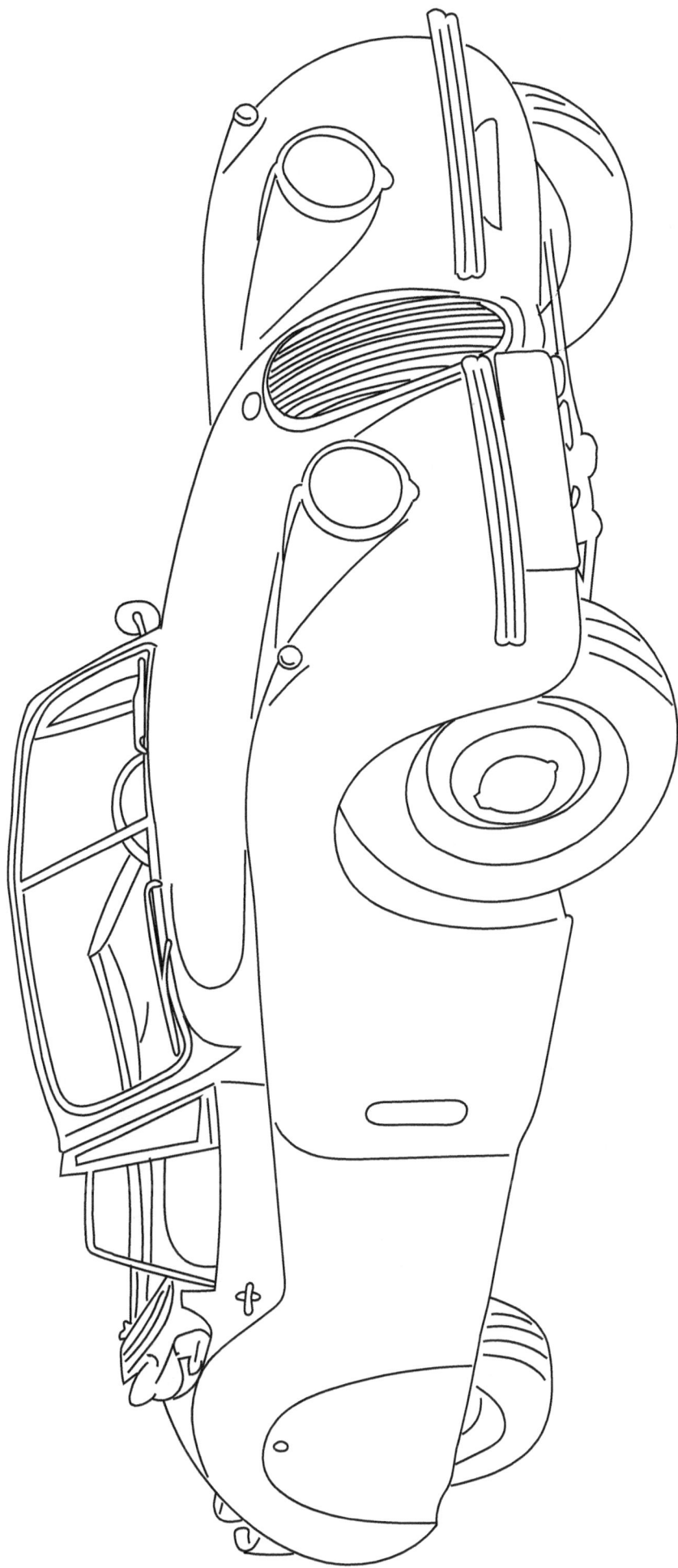

1953 Jaguar XK

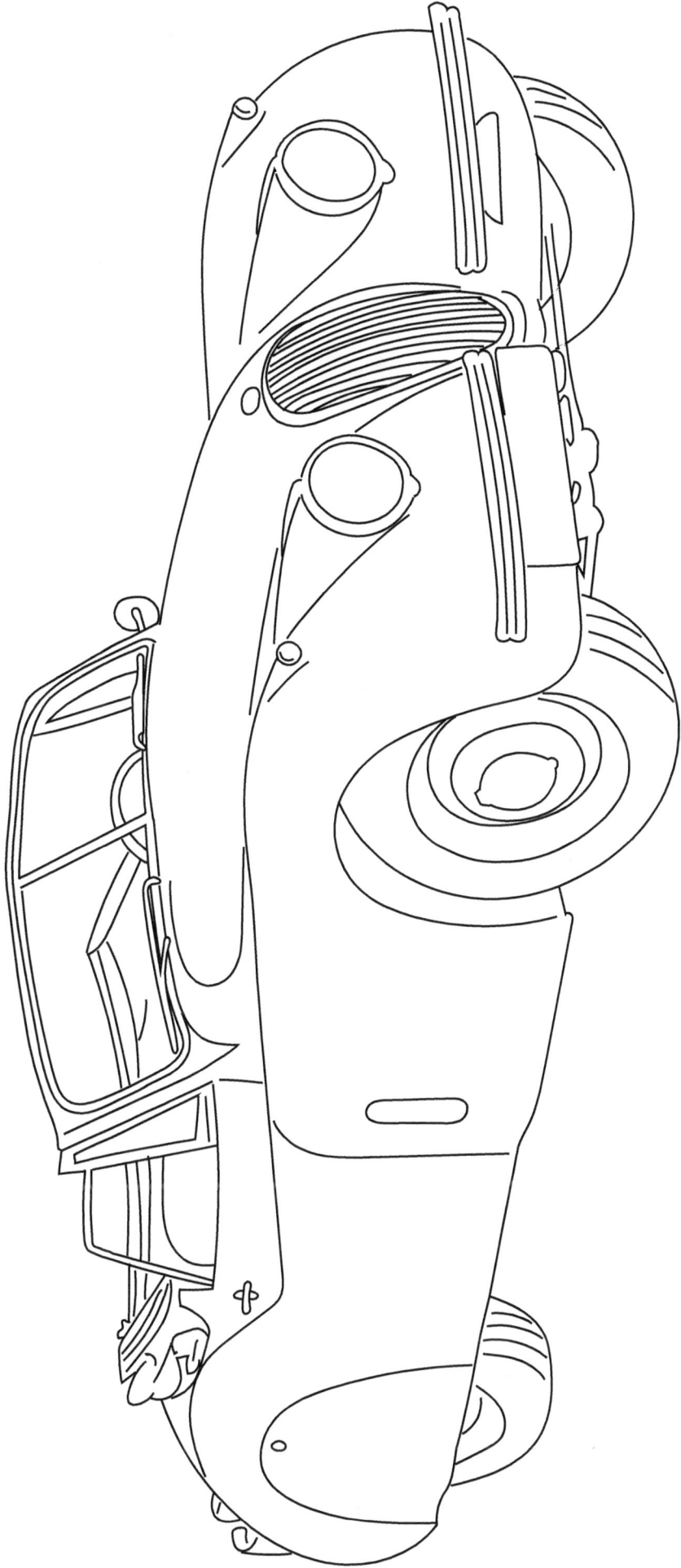

1953 Jaguar XK

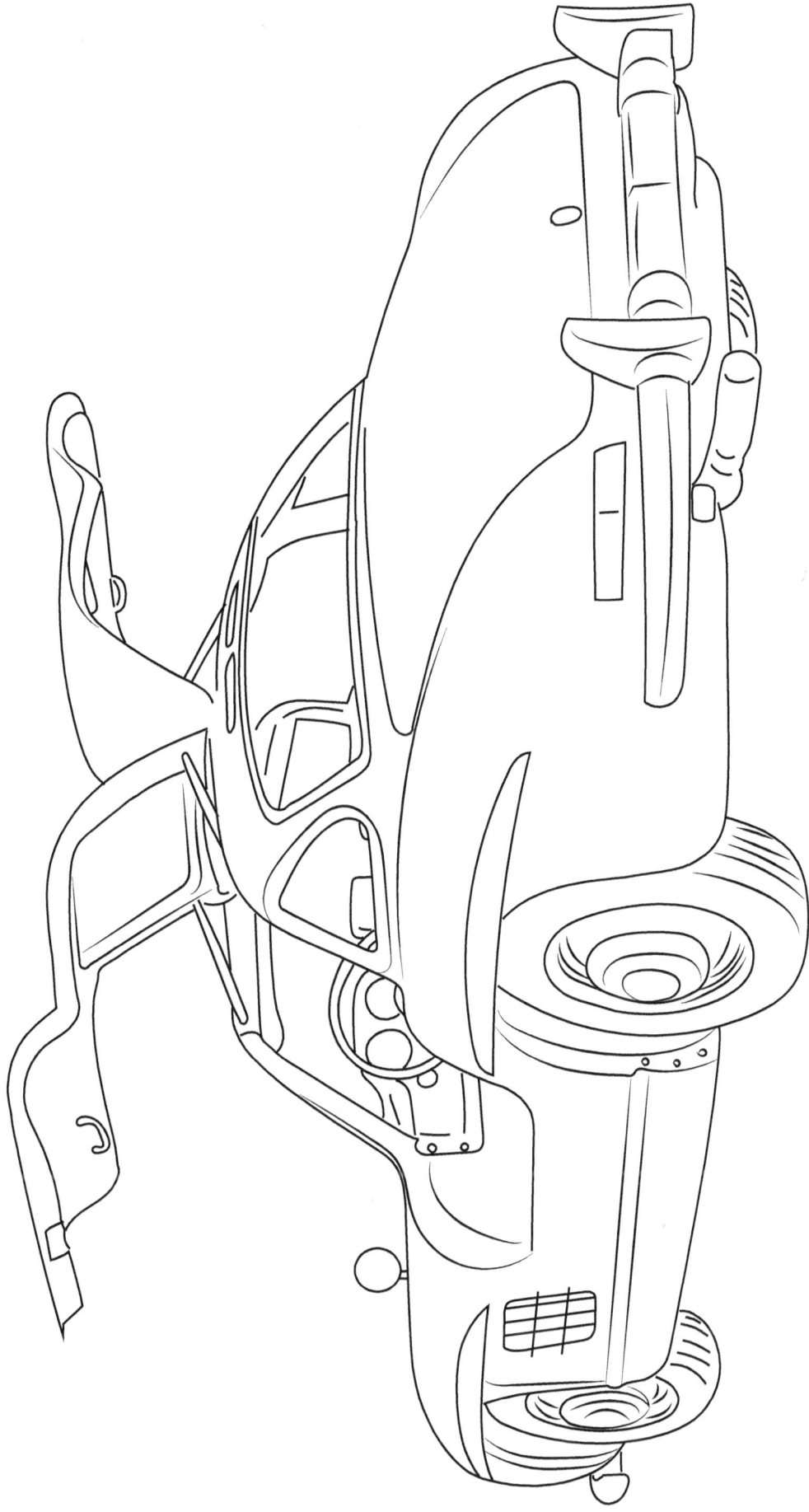

1955 Mercedes Benz 300SL Gullwing Coupe

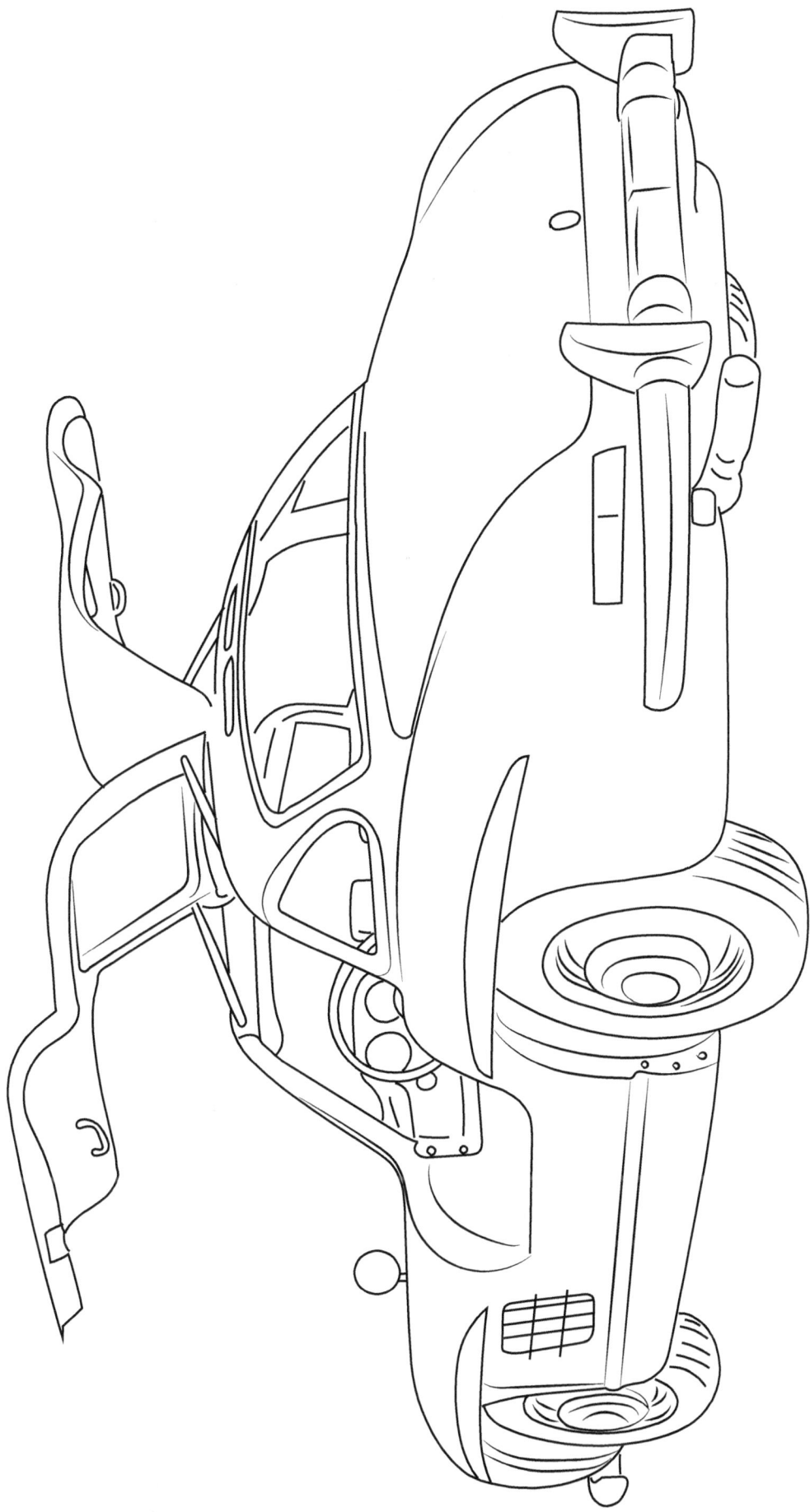

1955 Mercedes Benz 300SL Gullwing Coupe

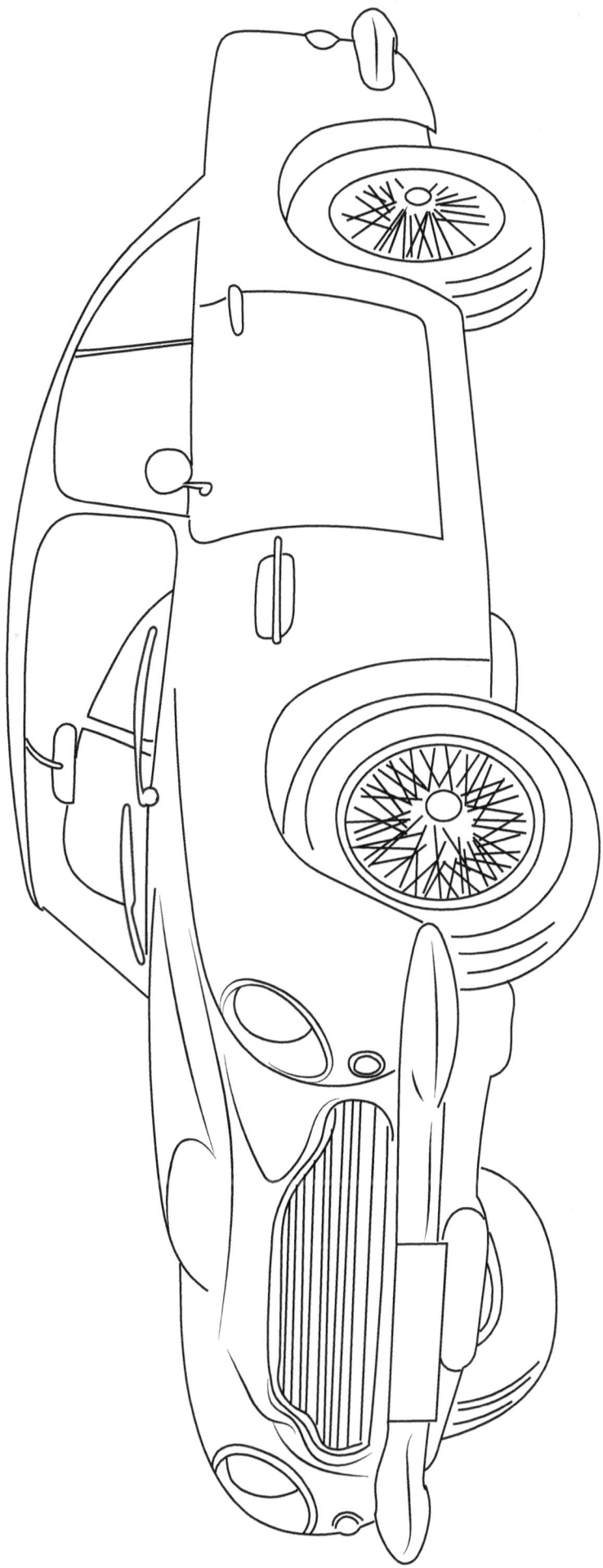

1959 Aston Martin DB4 GT Zagato

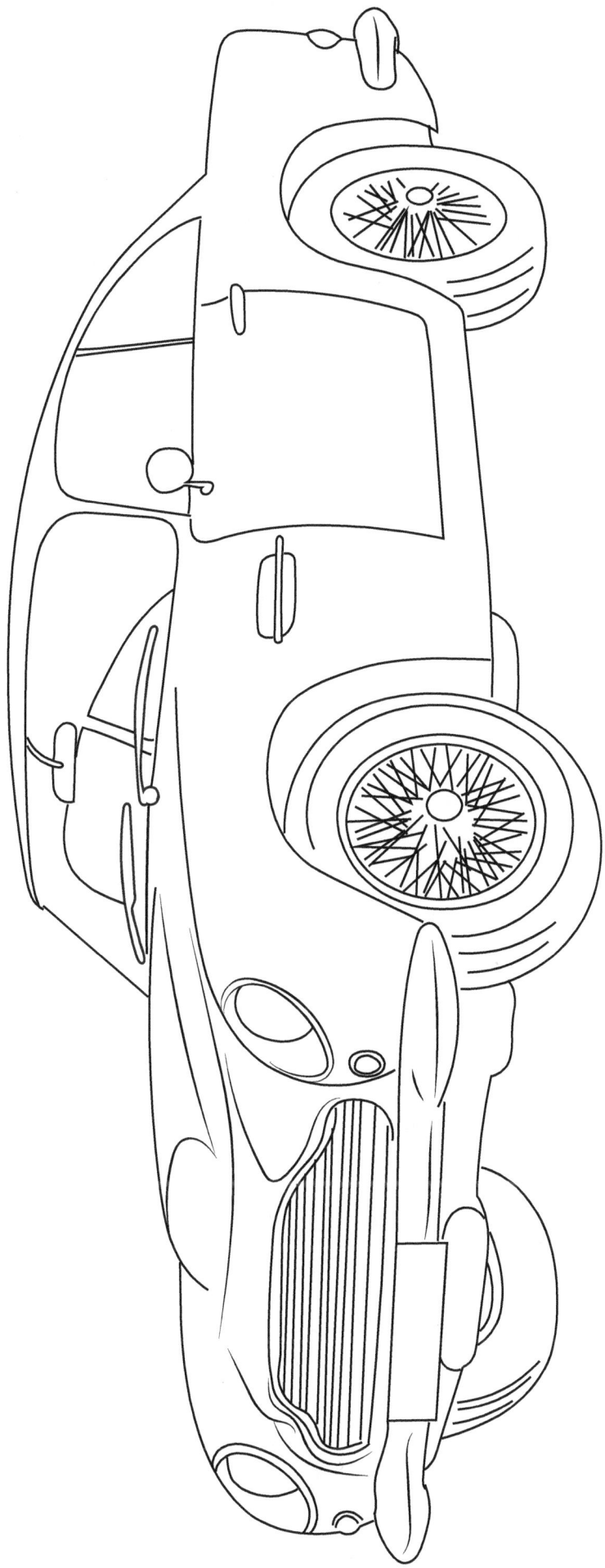

1959 Aston Martin DB4 GT Zagato

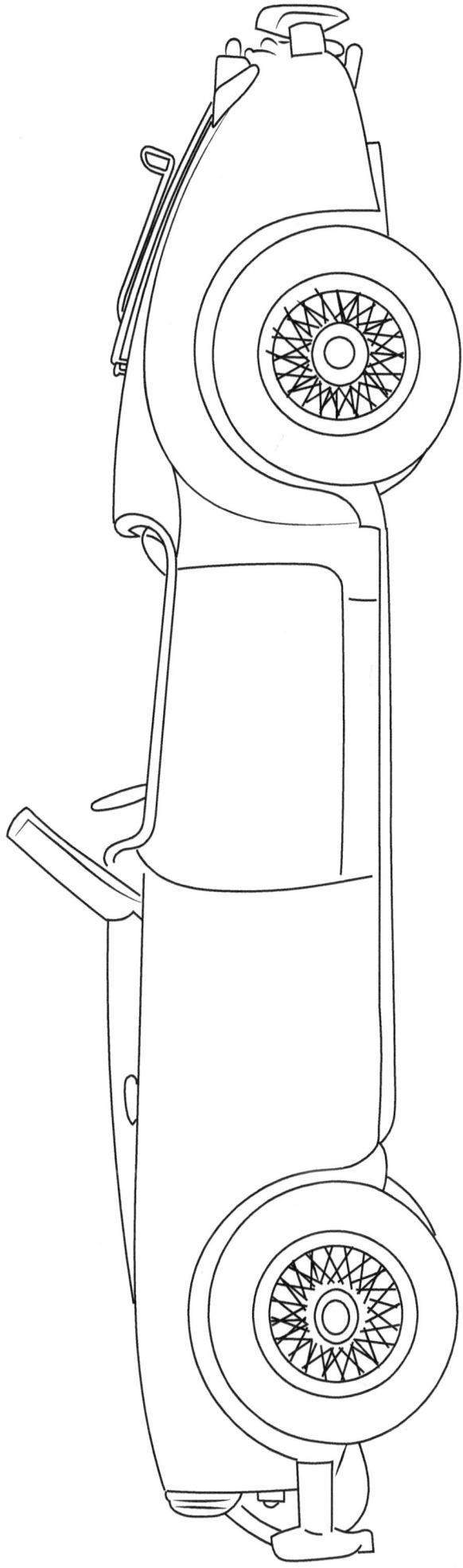

1959 MG MGS 1500

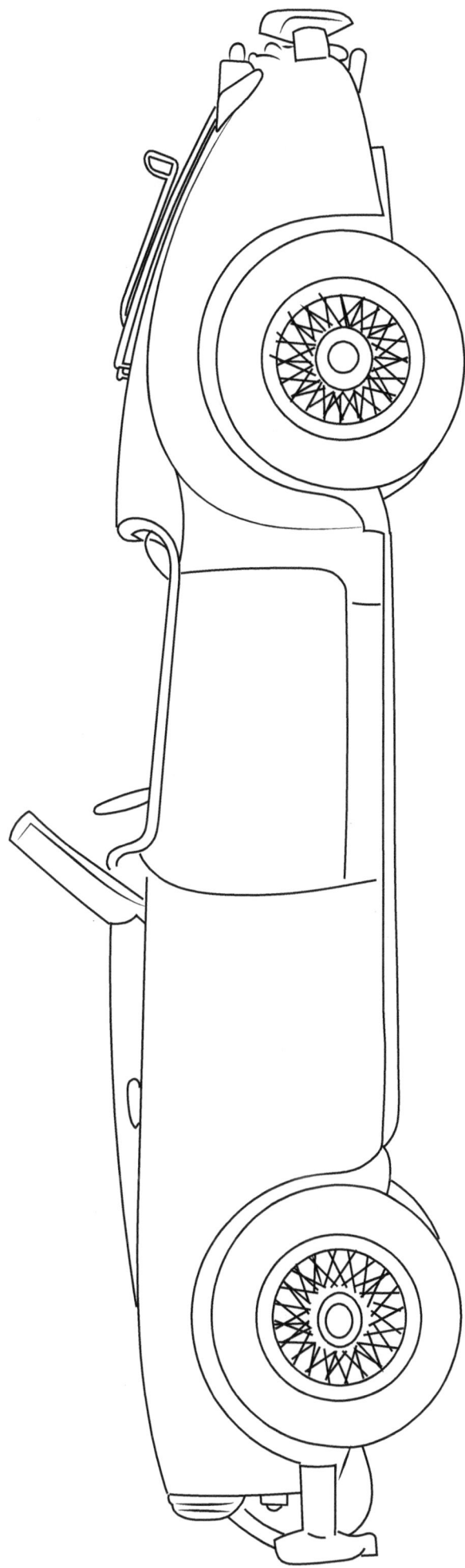

1959 MG MGS 1500